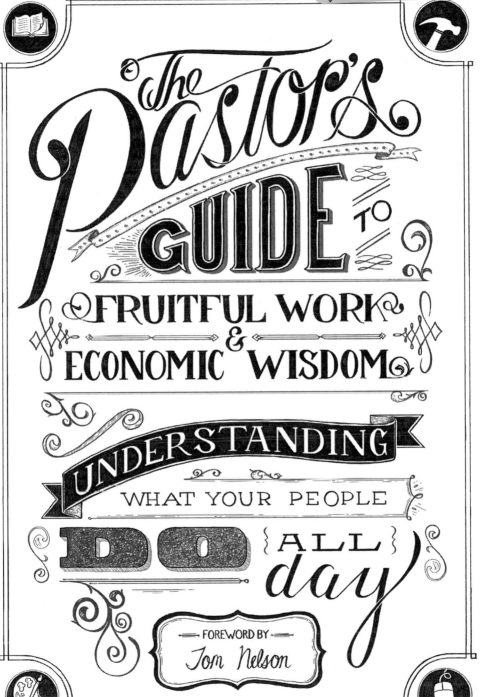

The Pastor's GUIDE TO FRUITFUL WORK & ECONOMIC WISDOM

UNDERSTANDING WHAT YOUR PEOPLE DO {ALL} day

FOREWORD BY
Tom Nelson

The Pastor's Guide to Fruitful Work & Economic Wisdom:
Understanding What Your People Do All Day

Permission was granted for use of the "Made for Discipleship" essay from the following source: Charlie Self, "Flourishing Churches & Communities," preface (Oikonomia Series, Acton Institute, Grand Rapids: Christian Library Press, 2012). Permission was granted for use of the "Made for Community" essay from the following source: David Wright, "How God Makes the World a Better Place," part 4, chap. 5 (Oikonomia Series, Acton Institute, Grand Rapids: Christian Library Press, 2012).

Edited by Drew Cleveland and Greg Forster

Cover design by Joseph Wilson

Interior design by Tyra Baumler

CONTENTS

FOREWORD

I remember a wise mentor repeatedly reminding me of the need for leaders to have clarity of purpose and mission. One of his favorite phrases still rings loudly in my mind. *"If there is a mist in the pulpit, there will be a fog in the pew."* Good advice for sure, but what happens when there is a fog in the pulpit?

A few years into my pastoral ministry, I was forced to confront this compelling question. In spite of my pastoral diligence, packed schedule, and the best of intentions, there was a dense fog in my pulpit. I faced an inconvenient truth. I had been committing pastoral malpractice. Sadly, I had spent the minority of my time equipping my congregation for what they had been called by God to do the majority of their lives. Rather than narrowing the Sunday to Monday gap that many in my congregation were experiencing, I had actually perpetuated a widening gap. My impoverished theological vision was impairing our congregation's spiritual formation, our contribution to the common good, and our local church's gospel mission.

Pastoral repentance was the necessary next step. I am most grateful for a gracious congregation that was ready to forgive my failings and move forward, guided by a more robust theology of vocation. In his insightful book, "Christian Mission in the Modern World," John Stott makes the point that we must begin with vocation. But what does this mean? I believe it means that we must see the entire biblical text as a coherent narrative of creation, fall, redemption, and consummation, revealing God's design and desire for human flourishing. I also believe we must regain the transforming truth that the gospel speaks into every nook and cranny of human existence, calling us to discipleship in all spheres of life.

The Holy Scriptures inform us that as image bearers, we have been created by a working God with work in mind. That means, in part, we have been created with community and collaboration in mind – *work is not an isolated activity, but an interdependent one.* We presently live in a broken and fallen world where our work is not what it ought to be. The good news is that through the redemptive work of Jesus, the work we do and the workplaces we inhabit are profoundly changed by the gospel.

For those of us who have been called to the pastoral vocation, the implications of a more robust theology of vocation not only reshape our thinking, but also our pastoral priorities and practices. Our reading diet will adjust to better understand the Monday world of our congregation. Our preaching will look and sound different. Our discipleship and spiritual formation pathways will take on a more integral shape and a new transformational influence. A pastoral visit to the workplace of a congregation member will become as common as a visit to the hospital. Our growing understanding of the church's mission in the world will enthusiastically embrace our congregation's everyday work life. We will grasp with new conviction and passion that economic flourishing matters and that a primary work of the church is the church at work. Empowered and guided by the Holy Spirit, the local church we serve will be more faithful to Christ and more effective in furthering the common good.

This is why my heart leaps with joy that you are carving out time to read and reflect on the wise and thoughtful words contained in the following pages of this very important book. Over the last several years, I have had the pleasure of spending time with many of the authors who penned these biblically informed and helpful chapters. I consider many of them friends and insightful conversational partners, and I appreciate how they continue to sharpen my life and help me be a more wise, effective, and faithful pastor.

One of the surprising joys of my life has been to see firsthand the good work The Kern Family Foundation is doing to foster human flourishing. I am most grateful for the many opportunities to roll up my sleeves and serve the Made to Flourish Network and the Oikonomia Network. I pray that this book in no small way will inform your mind, stretch your imagination, stir your heart, and change your life, as well as that of the congregation you serve. May our churches be all Jesus desires them to be, and may we who have been called to the pastoral vocation one day hear:

"Well done good and faithful servant, enter into the joy of your Master."

Tom Nelson, Senior Pastor
Christ Community Church
Leawood, Kan.

Introduction
WHAT ARE PEOPLE MADE FOR?

"The 98 percent of Christians who are not in church-paid work are, on the whole, not equipped or envisioned for mission ... in 95 percent of their waking lives. What a tragic waste of human potential!"

This sobering evaluation of the church's struggle to equip people to live as disciples of Christ in all of life was made from the podium at the most recent meeting of the Lausanne Congress, in 2010. Lausanne is by far the largest and most influential gathering of evangelical Christians in the world. The speaker was Mark Greene, executive director of the London Institute for Contemporary Christianity.[1]

Human potential – what is that? *What are we made for?* People today ask the same questions they have always asked: Is there meaning to what I do all day? What purposes are worth striving for? The gospel speaks to these questions, so why is it rare for us to think about the church in terms of human potential?

Even at its best, the task of the pastor is a hard one. And pastors are not exactly showered with recognition for the indispensable contribution they make to our lives. As a result, anything that makes the pastoral task harder is not likely to find many takers.

But engaging with big questions like "What are we made for?" is not something that makes the pastoral task harder. It *is* the pastoral task. Helping people do fruitful work and learn economic wisdom is central to the church's job of making disciples, loving our neighbors, and empowering the poor.

Greene made the case to the over 4,000 Lausanne delegates that most churches have a broken model of pastoral ministry. Our model, he said, ought to be "to equip the people of God for fruitful mission in all of their lives." However, the model that predominates in churches throughout the world is "to recruit the people of God to use some of their leisure time to join the missionary initiatives of church-paid workers." The calling of God, the front line in the spiritual war, is confined to what goes on in the church building and in special religious works. Only the clergy are in "full-time ministry." Too many churches simply ignore the spiritual significance of the activities that take up 95 percent of life for 98 percent of the population.

---

[1] Mark Greene, "Mark Greene at Lausanne Conference 2010" (The London Institute of Contemporary Christianity, 2010), http://www.youtube.com/watch?v=Owuab_M5L3Y.

TWO MODELS OF PASTORAL MINISTRY

The Model We Have
To recruit the people of God
to use some of their leisure time
to join the missionary initiatives
of church-paid workers.

The Model We Need
To equip the people of God
for fruitful mission
in all of their lives.

Source: Mark Greene, speech to the Lausanne Conference 2010.

The key missing piece is work. People spend most of their time working, once you add up activities in the home, in the workplace, and elsewhere. If we do not teach people to view their work, and the whole economic sphere of activity, as integral to the way God wants them to live, Christianity is reduced from a full-time way of life to nothing more than a leisure-time activity. Our walk with Jesus becomes something we squeeze into our schedules when we are not working. "So the workplace agenda is not some little thing on the side," said Greene. "The church's failure to embrace the workplace challenge is a symptom of a much deeper problem that affects almost every area of the church's mission to the world."

Connecting pastoral ministry to work is not about helping people become more successful in worldly terms. It's about helping them become more "successful" the way God defines success: walking with Jesus, practicing Christian virtues, loving their neighbors, and contributing to the good of those around them. Everyone from the CEO to the line worker, from the doctor working on a cancer cure to the school janitor working on a piece of gum stuck to the cafeteria floor, needs to live out the meaning of their lives through their work.

This is a time of great hope for renewal. When Greene spoke in 2010, there was already a large and growing movement of Christians determined to reconnect the church with the world of work and the economy. Since then, that movement has exploded into the larger consciousness of the church. Work and economics will be at the forefront of the church's attention in the coming generation.

Theologian R. Paul Stevens points out that Jesus and the Apostles made it clear that the kingdom of God manifests itself in all of life. Work and economics seem to have been a central concern for them. Consider how, as Stevens shows, the overwhelming majority of Jesus' public appearances and parables in the Gospels, as well as the divine interventions in the book of Acts, occur in the marketplace:

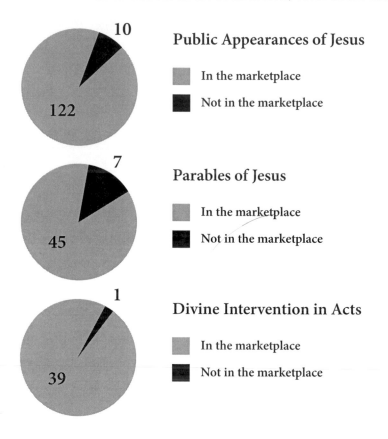

Source: R. Paul Stevens, "Work Matters: Lessons from Scripture," Wm. B. Eerdmans, 2012, 134.

Stevens writes that Jesus was an entrepreneur, and the new enterprise he was founding and building was the kingdom of God.[2] He did not ask people to sign their names on a list, then go on living exactly as before. He recruited people to join his venture and build a new way of life. How might that change our perspective on what the Kingdom is and how we, as his disciples, build it?

---

[2] R. Paul Stevens, "Work Matters: Lessons from Scripture" (Grand Rapids: Wm. B. Eerdmans Publishing Co., 2012), 135.

How might that perspective on the Kingdom, in turn, change our model of pastoral ministry? If the Kingdom must manifest itself in the public square, in work, and in economics (as well as other places), then the church building is not the front line of the spiritual war. It is more like a base camp or field hospital; the front lines are in homes, workplaces, and communities. The calling of God is in every arena of service, and all believers are in full-time service to Christ from the moment they become Christians.

Tom Nelson, in his book on how the idea of vocation transforms pastoral ministry, draws our attention to the seamless connection between our work and the three things that abide: faith, hope, and love. Paul writes, "We give thanks to God always for all of you ... remembering before our God and Father your work of faith and labor of love and steadfastness of hope in our Lord Jesus Christ" (1 Thessalonians 1:2-3). Nelson comments: "These virtues are ensconced in the language of work and labor. The rest of the letter tells us that the *work of faith, labor of love*, and *steadfastness of hope* Paul has in mind was not confined to some other world contemplative spirituality, but rather to real-world vocational life."[3]

"Real-world vocational life" – that is the 95 percent of life for 98 percent of people that the gospel must speak to. It is the world of human potential, the world where we strive to become what we were made for.

Because work is most of life, work must be central to a Christian understanding of what it means to be human and what makes life worth living. Otherwise, most of what we do all day remains arbitrary and meaningless even in light of the gospel, and faith cannot provide people with a satisfying and sustainable life. We cannot accept that outcome if Christianity is what the Bible says it is – an integrated, 24/7 walk with Christ, not the leisure-time activity it has become for too many people.

As the essays in this volume will show, the Bible speaks at length about work and economics. Our daily labor is the subject of extensive scriptural concern; passages running from Genesis 1 through Revelation 22 teach us to view our work as central to the meaning of our lives. We are taught to view our work as service to God and neighbor, to work diligently in an honest calling, and to persevere under the challenges of a fallen and broken world. Work is one of the most important tools God uses to transform our character spiritually – work is a chisel for sculpting the self, as author Lester DeKoster puts it.[4]

Work is not only personal and individual; it is also public and social. Thus, the Bible speaks to the vast web of relationships and cultural assumptions within which we work – what is now called "the economy." These structures of property

---

[3] Tom Nelson, "Work Matters: Connecting Sunday Worship to Monday Work" (Wheaton: Crossway, 2011), 191.
[4] Lester DeKoster, "Work: The Meaning of Your Life," 2nd ed. (Grand Rapids: Christian's Library Press, 2010).

and economic exchange are the necessary context for our labor, and the gospel cannot speak to work without creating implications for how we organize the economic life of our civilization. Biblical teaching implies support for: the rule of law and equal protection of all people's rights to work, own, buy, sell, and build; setting public expectations of virtuous behavior and value creation; personal responsibility for well-being; helping those in need get connected to work; and generous support for those who are unable to work.

Greene is right that connecting pastoral ministry to work and the economy is "not some little thing on the side." It "goes right to the heart" of the pastor's task, shining the light of the gospel into that 95 percent of life for 98 percent of people. It shows us what we were made for. The movement to reclaim Christianity from its status as a leisure-time activity is already well underway. We hope this volume will help more pastors discover how they can make their churches part of the solution.

Made for
LOVE

Michael Wittmer

What are we made for? This is the question that defines our daily lives, even if we don't realize it. Effective gospel ministry involves helping people come to understand what they were made for and live lives that reflect their true purpose. However, as this eloquent yet plainspoken essay from Michael Wittmer argues, it can be very hard for pastors to keep this at the center of the local church's culture and practice. Too many churches have wandered into ways of thinking, speaking, and acting that are at odds with this mission. If we truly believe that we were made to love God, and that the local church is called to help people build their lives around this truth, a movement of reformation is needed.

Michael Wittmer is a professor of systematic theology and the director of the Center for Christian Worldview at Grand Rapids Theological Seminary in Grand Rapids, Mich. If you like this essay, check out his books "Becoming Worldly Saints" and "Heaven Is a Place on Earth," in which he shows the dramatic consequences of Christian faith for every aspect of life on earth – both the earth of the present age and the "new earth" of the age to come. His other books include "Despite Doubt," "The Last Enemy," "Christ Alone," and "Don't Stop Believing." Wittmer also serves as pulpit supply for churches in western Michigan, is a visiting professor at Asia Baptist Theological Seminary, and composes three devotionals each month for the radio ministry "Our Daily Journey."

The highest purpose of life is to love God. If you're a pastor, you may not find that statement surprising or challenging. Yet many evangelical churches today aren't doing all they can to help Christians live into the fullness of this purpose, and help the broader human community discover it.

A large part of a pastor's job is to regularly remind people that they are put on Earth to know and love God. If you are a good pastor, you continually search for memorable ways to register this point. You might cite the opening prayer of Augustine's "Confessions:" "You have made us for yourself, and our heart is restless until it rests in you."[5] Or you might quote the answer to the first question of the "Westminster Shorter Catechism," "Man's chief end is to glorify God, and enjoy him forever."[6] Unlike everything else God has made, humans are natural creatures with a supernatural end. Nothing down here can ultimately satisfy. It's not supposed to.

You might illustrate this point with Ecclesiastes. Here is a man, presumably Solomon, who had everything and a little more. He searched for satisfaction in wine, projects, gardens, music, and excessive wealth. He said, "I became greater by far than anyone in Jerusalem before me. ... I denied myself nothing my eyes desired; I refused my heart no pleasure." And yet he concluded, "Meaningless! Meaningless! ... Utterly meaningless! Everything is meaningless" (Ecclesiastes 2:9-10; 1:2).

You might update this example with a contemporary Solomon. Tom Brady is a Super Bowl-winning quarterback who married a supermodel and recently built a $20 million house that is surrounded by a moat. But it's still not enough. Brady confessed during an interview: "Why do I have three Super Bowl rings and still think there's something greater out there for me? I mean, maybe a lot of people would say, 'Hey man, this is what is.' I reached my goal, my dream, my life. Me, I think, 'God, it's got to be more than this.' I mean this isn't, this can't be what it's all cracked up to be."

The interviewer asked, "What's the answer?" Brady responded, "I wish I knew. I wish I knew."[7]

You might exhort your congregation to listen to these voices calling from the top of the ladder of success. Some in your church might be halfway up, while others are just beginning their climb. But as they put their foot on the next rung, or even the first rung, they need to know that no matter how this goes – whether

---

[5] Augustine, Confessions I.1, trans. Henry Chadwick (New York: Oxford University Press, 1991), 3.

[6] "Westminster Shorter Catechism," 1st ed., 1011.

[7] Daniel Schorn, "Tom Brady: The Winner," CBSNews.com, November 2005, http://www.cbsnews.com/news/transcript-tom-brady-part-3/.

they make it all the way to the top, or whether they become stranded midway – the ladder is not the thing that will ultimately satisfy. Take it from Augustine, Solomon, and Tom. The only thing that can possibly satisfy us is God.

The application of this message seems obvious. If we are put on Earth to know and love God, then we must make time to know and love God. So begin every day with Scripture and prayer. Make corporate worship a priority. We all are crazy busy these days, yet we create space in our schedule for what we care about most. Thank God when your daily devotions seem inconvenient. When you make time for God when you would rather be doing something else, you are telling God in unmistakable terms that you love him. So rejoice when your faith costs you something. Gladly pay it, and keep the receipt. It's proof that your faith in Christ is real.

What Does It Mean to Be Human?

These points on loving God are the bread and butter of gospel ministry, and I make them all when I preach. We must repeatedly remind our congregation that God and his kingdom are like a treasure hidden in a field or a pearl of great price, and it is worth selling everything we have to buy that treasure or get that pearl (Matthew 13:44-46). As Jesus asked, "What good will it be for someone to gain the whole world, yet forfeit their soul? Or what can anyone give in exchange for their soul?" (Matthew 16:26).

We must regularly say that God is our top priority, and clear our schedules so we can hear his Word and speak to him in prayer. But is this enough? If this is all the instruction we give about loving God, we can leave a perilously wrong impression. When the only way to love God is to read our Bible and pray, we inadvertently tell people three dangerous things:

1. We check off God.

God must be number one in our life, but if that is all he is, then we might think we can check him off our list. We have our devotions first thing in the morning. Check! The rest of the day is for us. We give God a tithe before we spend a dime on anything else. Check! The rest of our money is for us. We set aside the first day of the week to worship him at church. Check! The rest of the week is for us.

When we check off God, we inevitably fall into a second error:

2. We compartmentalize our lives.

Our people know God cares about the eternal, spiritual stuff, but they don't always think he cares about temporal, physical matters. They know they should store up "treasure in heaven" (Matthew 6:19-21), and they assume they do this only when they do something overtly spiritual such as read their Bible, pray, or tell others about Jesus. They are not always aware that God also rewards the mundane parts of life, such as how they treat their spouse, talk to their kids, or do their jobs (Colossians 3:23-24).

And sometimes they have learned this from us. I have heard more than one pastor say, "The only reason we are still on this planet is to lead souls to Christ." Well, if this is the only reason we are still here, then it is hard to justify doing anything else besides evangelism. And it is hard to explain why we should do these other things well, because ultimately they don't really count. As one pastor explained:

> The bottom line is that we are to put spiritual values above temporal values. Serving God and being obedient to him ought to be more important to us than anything else we do, including fishing, golfing, hunting, gardening, our career, clothes, houses, lands, etc. These things are not wrong, but they are not to be the primary focus and priorities of our life. God wants and demands first place!

This pastor is right that God must be more important than anything else, but this hard division between spiritual and temporal activities is a back door to worldliness. There are two ways to become worldly. The obvious way is to care so much about the things of this world that we never make time for God. The other is to focus so much on God that we never integrate our love for him with our life in this world. We do shoddy or even unethical work because we do not think these worldly activities matter.

Rather than viewing temporal activities as nothing more than threats to the supremacy of God, why not view them as opportunities to live for him? What might happen if Christians realize that everything they do matters to God? Consider the Great Recession. What if just the Christian homebuyers had remained content to live within their means? What if just the Christian mortgage brokers had refused to offer subprime loans they knew the applicants could not afford? What if just the Christian financiers had refused to slice toxic mortgages and repackage them to unsuspecting customers? What if Christians in government had been working to change the policy and regulatory environment that encourages and incentivizes these irresponsible behaviors? If only those who claimed to follow Christ had lived as if he claimed their lives, the world might not have suffered the economic collapse we are still climbing out of.

Christians who compartmentalize their lives fall into a third error. They logically but mistakenly conclude:

3. Much of life doesn't count.

One of the most popular books of all time is "The Purpose Driven Life." This best-selling book has been used by the Lord, yet it also supplies evidence that evangelicals tend to separate their human and Christian lives. This book has inspired many, though it barely begins to answer the question raised in its subtitle, "What on earth am I here for?" It says we are here to accomplish five purposes: worship, ministry, fellowship, evangelism, and discipleship.[8] Of these, worship is the only category that is broad enough to cover all of life. Author Rick Warren rightly explains, "Every activity can be transformed into an act of worship when you do it for the praise, glory, and pleasure of God." Yet Warren says the way to do everything for the glory of God is by "doing it for Jesus and by carrying on a continual conversation with him while you do it."[9] Do our human activities have value in their own right, as obedience to the creation mandate of Genesis 1:28 and 2:15, or do they only count when we sanctify them by keeping a running dialogue with Jesus?

The other four purposes in "The Purpose Driven Life" are exclusively Christian activities. This is obviously the case for evangelism and discipleship, but even fellowship and ministry are limited to the life of the church. Warren declares that fellowship is "participating in the fellowship of God's eternal family" and that "mission" (by which he means evangelism), rather than "ministry," describes our relationship to the unsaved world.[10] He mentions that God gives us natural gifts, such as "artistic ability, architectural ability, administering, baking," and so forth, but he only describes how we might use these gifts in the church. He explains, "God has a place in his church where your specialties can shine and you can make a difference."[11]

"The Purpose Driven Life" concludes by summarizing its five purposes for life and declaring, "A great commitment to the Great Commandment and the Great Commission will make you a great Christian."[12] I am all for being a great Christian, but most of our lives do not fit into exclusively Christian categories. C. S. Lewis observed that coming to Jesus did not change so much of *what* he did, but *how* he did it. He wrote, "Before I became a Christian I do not think I fully realized that one's life, after conversion, would inevitably consist in doing most of the same things one had been doing before, one hopes, in a new spirit, but still the same things."[13] Christian or not, we are going to spend much of our lives hanging out with family and friends, mowing the lawn and washing the car, cooking

[8] Rick Warren, "The Purpose Driven Life" (Grand Rapids: Zondervan, 2002), 306. Warren does mention in passing that caring for creation is "a part of our purpose," (44) but in the next chapter he blunts this insight by stating that this world is temporary, so we should not be overly concerned with it. (47-52)
[9] Ibid., 67. Warren also helpfully says, "Every human activity, except sin, can be done for God's pleasure if you do it with an attitude of praise. You can wash dishes, repair a machine, sell a product, write a computer program, grow a crop, and raise a family for the glory of God." (74)
[10] Ibid., 120, 281.
[11] Ibid., 242-44.
[12] Ibid., 306.
[13] C. S. Lewis, "Learning in War-Time," in "The Weight of Glory" (San Francisco: Harper San Francisco, 1980), 51.

dinner and cleaning up, and any number of things that we do, not because we are Christian, but simply because we are human.[14]

What does the Bible say about such things? To find out, we must search for the meaning of life where the Bible begins – with creation, not redemption. Rather than starting at the end of the biblical story and asking, "I'm *saved*, so what is the meaning of my *Christian* life?" what if we started with creation and asked, "I'm *imago* Dei, so what is the meaning of my *human* life?" We would generate a much broader list of purposes, as broad as life itself. The story of creation tells us that we are on Earth to love God, serve others (Genesis 1:27), responsibly cultivate the Earth (Genesis 1:28; 2:15), and rest every seven days (Genesis 2:1-3).

Everything we could ever do easily falls into one of these categories. Most things fall into more than one of these overlapping categories, causing us to do each of them by doing the others. We love God by serving others and cultivating the earth; we serve others by loving God and developing culture; and we take better care of the earth when we obey God and seek our neighbor's good.

These all-encompassing creation categories bring meaning to every area of life. Our "life on earth" is more than "just the dress rehearsal before the real production." It is not merely "the staging area, the preschool, the tryout for your life in eternity." It is not just "the practice workout before the actual game; the warm-up lap before the race begins."[15] This life is the real deal. It counts.

Starting with creation also enables us to see that our human and Christian lives are not at war. If redemption restores creation, then the whole point of being a redeemed Christian is to become a more flourishing human. Jesus did not come to this planet to obliterate our humanity, turning us into angelic beings focused solely on spiritual activities. Jesus is fully God and fully human. He is zero percent angel. And so he came to cross out our sin and empower us to thrive in every part of our human lives. Everything we do matters to God.

Tension: Pearl and Yeast

Living to love God as *humans* requires us to wrestle with a difficult tension. Jesus compared the kingdom of God to a treasure hidden in a field and a pearl of great price. Then in the same chapter, he told another parable: "The kingdom of heaven is like yeast that a woman took and mixed into about 60 pounds of flour until it worked all through the dough" (Matthew 13:33). Do you hear the tension

---

[14] To be fair, Warren himself sometimes speaks to these issues. In 2012, he preached a sermon series on the importance of work, titled "Doing Business with God," http://www.saddlebackresources.com/024300_Doing-Business-With-God-C3202.aspx. Concurrent with the series, thousands of workplace small groups at Saddleback studied a video series, "Christians in the Workplace," https://saddleback.com/mc/ms/6c146/.

[15] Warren, "The Purpose Driven Life," 36.

between these dueling parables? God and his kingdom are the pearl that is worth more than the world. But the Kingdom is also yeast that permeates the world and causes it to rise.

When you love someone, you tend to take an interest in what they love. Because I love my children, I know the names of more Nintendo characters and gymnastic flips than a grown man should. And because I love God, I must also love what he loves. What does God love? The world (John 3:16).

Do you feel the tension? We must love God more than the world, yet if we truly love God, we will also love the world on his behalf. God matters more than the world, but because he loves it, the world now matters.

We sing the hymn, "Turn your eyes upon Jesus, Look full in His wonderful face, and *the things of earth will grow strangely dim*, In the light of His glory and grace." This is a powerful statement of the Kingdom as a pearl, but I always want to add a second version of the chorus that emphasizes that the Kingdom is also yeast. "Turn your eyes upon Jesus, Look full in His wonderful face, and the things of earth will grow strangely *significant!*"

Here's the point: God must be more than merely our top priority. He must also permeate our lives. God and his kingdom are like the hub of a wheel, and the spokes that penetrate outward must transform every aspect of our lives. God cares deeply that we read our Bible, pray, worship, and support our local church; he also cares how we talk to our family, what we do for fun, and how we perform our jobs. Jesus is the Creator of all and the Redeemer of all, which means he is Lord of all. It all counts now (Colossians 1:15-20; 3:23-24).

The Reformers conveyed this truth with the notion of vocation, or calling. In their day, many in the church hierarchy reserved the term "calling" for priests, monks, and nuns who had left the world to serve God in a religious vocation. These highly committed men and women were particularly close to God, for they had aimed higher than marriage and money and had taken the vow of celibacy and poverty. Martin Luther tried to live this way and nearly lost his mind. How could he ever give up enough earthly pleasure to satisfy the impossibly high standards of a holy God? After years of wrestling with Scripture and his own conscience, Luther finally discovered the Reformation insight that he was justified by faith alone. He could never do enough to meet God's righteous requirements, but he did not have to. Jesus' substitutionary sacrifice had secured Luther's salvation, which freed him to open his life to others.

Soon afterward, Luther wrote "The Freedom of a Christian," a "small book" that "contains the whole of Christian life in a brief form, provided you grasp its meaning."[16] Luther explained that when he was a monk, he spent all of his resources trying to save his own soul. Once he knew he was secure, he suddenly had a lot of time on his hands. Why not use this freedom to serve others?

Luther took this to heart, and a few years later he married. He had three reasons: He wanted to spite the pope, produce grandchildren for his father, and seal his witness to the Reformation (he assumed he would be killed within a year). A truckload of nuns came to Wittenberg, hidden in whiskey barrels (clearly, they were German nuns). Luther found husbands for all of them except one, and after many failed attempts, he stepped forward and offered to marry her himself. His friends were not fond of the much younger Katherine, and even Luther admitted, "I am not infatuated, though I cherish my wife ... God has given her to me and other women have worse faults." Though Luther may not have much to teach us regarding how a husband should praise his wife, his marriage, which soon enough became an exemplary Christian union, supplied the template for future Protestant notions of the Christian life. No longer would one have to forgo marriage and leave the world to please God. Now anyone could please God right where they were, as long as they saw their matrimonial and worldly duties as a divine calling.

Luther explained in a sermon on Matthew 6:24-34:

> To serve God simply means to do what God has commanded and not to do what God has forbidden. And if only we would accustom ourselves properly to this view, the entire world would be full of service to God, not only the churches but also the home, the kitchen, the cellar, the workshop, and the field of townsfolk and farmers. For it is certain that God would have not only the church and world order but also the house order established and upheld. All, therefore, who serve the latter purpose – father and mother first, then the children, and finally the servants and neighbors – are jointly serving God; for so He wills and commands.
>
> In the light of this view of the matter a poor maid should have the joy in her heart of being able to say: "Now I am cooking, making the bed, sweeping the house. Who has commanded me to do these things? My master and mistress have. Who has given them this authority over me? God has. Very well, then it must be true that I am serving not them alone but also God in heaven and that God must be pleased with my service. How could I possibly be more blessed? Why, my service is equal to cooking for God in heaven!"
>
> In this way a man could be happy and of good cheer in all his trouble and labor; and if he accustomed himself to look at his service and calling

---

[16] Martin Luther, "The Freedom of a Christian," in "Martin Luther's Basic Theological Writings," 2nd ed., ed. Timothy F. Lull and William R. Russell (Minneapolis: Fortress Press, 2005), 392.

in this way, nothing would be distasteful to him. But the devil opposes this point of view tooth and nail, to keep one from coming to this joy and to cause everybody to have a special dislike for what he should do and is commanded to do. So the devil operates in order to make sure that people do not love their work and no service be rendered to God.[17]

Theologian Herman Bavinck noticed Luther's emphasis on living for Jesus where and as you are, and concluded the Reformation was a "Reformation of the natural." Rather than continue the medieval call to rise beyond this world, the Reformers urged their followers to stay in the world and reform it.[18]

Pastor, do the people under your care understand that their entire life is an opportunity to love God? Or do they mistakenly suppose that only pastors and missionaries are in "full-time ministry?" (As if the rest are merely part-time.) My father's pastor once asked him to strip the wax off the floor of the church's restrooms. The pastor wanted him to do it soon, so he said working on the church's restrooms would be doing the Lord's work. Drawing a division between "the Lord's work" and other work creates an inappropriate hierarchy, setting those who do "the Lord's work" above those who don't.

I have three brothers who work in various businesses. One pastor told my dad that he must be happy to know that one of his sons is doing something of eternal significance. That would be me! I'm glad for the compliment, but what an awful thing to say! Aren't businesspeople also doing the Lord's work? Didn't my father serve the Lord just as much when he plowed snow and filled potholes for the street department as when he worked on the church's restrooms?

We need each other to do our callings as unto the Lord (Colossians 3:23-24). My father needs his pastor to study the Word, preach it faithfully, and visit him when he is sick. His pastor needs my father to clear the roads in winter, or he can't get to church to do his calling. And they both need businessmen such as my brothers to create jobs, or there would be no money to have a church, pay the pastor, or send missionaries. Religious callings are unique and indispensable, but they are not necessarily better. Luther explained:

> God cannot bear to see anyone neglect the duties of his calling or station in life in order to imitate the works of the saints. If therefore a married woman were to follow Anna in this respect, leave her husband and children, her home and parents in order to go on a pilgrimage, to pray, fast and go to church, she would do nothing else but tempt God, confound the

---

[17] "What Luther Says," comp. Ewald M. Plass (St. Louis: Concordia Publishing House, 1959), II:560.

[18] To read more of Herman Bavinck's understanding of the "Reformation of the natural," see Herman Bavinck, "The Catholicity of Christianity and the Church," Calvin Theological Journal 27 (November 1992): 220-51, doi: 10.1177/004056398704800117 and "Common Grace," Calvin Theological Journal 24 (April 1989): 35-65.

matrimonial estate with the state of widowhood, desert her own calling and do works belonging to others. This would be as much as walking on one's ears, putting a veil over one's feet and a boot on one's head, and turning all things upside down. Good works should be done, and you ought to pray and fast, but you must not thereby be kept from or neglect the duties of your calling and station.[19]

There is nothing so great that it can't be done sinfully (e.g., preaching a sermon for applause or a paycheck), and there is nothing so small that it can't earn God's reward. God rewards such "spiritual" activities as Bible reading, prayer, and making disciples, but he also rewards Christians who flip burgers and sweep the floor for the Lord. Yes, even fast food can be a divine calling, as anyone who has eaten at a Chick-Fil-A already knows.

Nineteenth century poet Gerard Manley Hopkins may have said it best. He wrote: "To lift up the hands in prayer gives God glory, but a man with a dungfork in his hand, a woman with a slop pail, give him glory too. He is so great that all things give him glory if you mean they should."[20] Pastors, let's mean they should.

REFLECTION QUESTIONS

1. Who is in full-time ministry? Which activities in the present world are of eternal significance? What do we do in everyday life that brings glory to God?

2. What impact does it have on our lives when we "check off" God? How often do people use church and religious activities to check God off their list?

3. How is the gospel a "pearl of great price," and how does that affect everyday life? How is the gospel "yeast mixed into the dough," and how does that affect everyday life?

---

[19] Martin Luther, "Sermons of Martin Luther: The Church Postils," Vol 1 and 2, ed. and trans. John Nicholas Lenker (Grand Rapids: Baker Books, 1995), 281.

[20] Gerard Manley Hopkins, "The Principle or Foundation," in "Gerard Manley Hopkins: The Major Works," ed. Catherine Phillips (New York: Oxford University Press, 2002), 292.

Made for
DISCIPLESHIP

Charlie Self

If we were made to love God, we cannot be content to express our love for God through a narrow set of special religious activities, separate from daily life and withdrawn from the world. We were made to live all of life as full-time disciples of Christ. As Charlie Self demonstrates in this short, but indelibly memorable excerpt from his book, "Flourishing Churches and Communities," to love God with all of our heart, soul, strength, and mind is not a separate activity we squeeze into our lives along with all our other activities. It is how we need to do everything. "Ministry" – service to God and neighbor that helps the world flourish – is what we do all day.

Charlie Self is a professor of church history at Assemblies of God Theological Seminary in Springfield, Mo. He served as a pastor for 30 years prior to entering the academy. He holds a B.A., M.A., and Ph.D. from the University of California, Santa Cruz and an M.A. from the Graduate Theological Union. He is a senior advisor at the Acton Institute and a member of the national advisory committee of the Oikonomia Network. He splits his time between Missouri and northern California, where he directed the establishment of the seminary's satellite campus in 2007. He is an active public speaker and appears frequently as "Dr. History" on a leading San Francisco talk radio program. If you like this excerpt, check out the full book, "Flourishing Churches and Communities," which introduces the full integration of faith with the world of work and economics from a Pentecostal perspective. Self's other books include "The Power of Faithful Focus" and "The Divine Dance."

Scotty is every pastor's dream of an ideal church member. A mechanic by trade, Scotty owns an independent shop in Campbell, Calif. – in the heart of Silicon Valley. He and his family are active in Bethel Church of San Jose, serving on committees and production teams, teaching, helping out with special-needs children, and enjoying fellowship with others. He is active in Christian bass-fishing tournaments, through which he has seen many come to Christ. He is cheerful, hardworking, and has a great reputation in the community. Scotty seeks to honor the Lord in all he does.

By most measures of Christian discipleship, Scotty is exactly what all churches need. He loves God, reads the Bible, and attends church faithfully, gives his money and time generously, and enjoys the respect of his colleagues and neighbors. Scotty is indeed an exemplary disciple – but there is more to this story!

What is missing from the discipleship accounts of most believers is the fact that Scotty's full-time "ministry" and greatest Kingdom service takes place during the 60-plus hours a week he and his wife, Patti, devote to their business. Scotty's Automotive is not merely a secular means to a sacred end. The business is the mission, contributing directly to the flourishing of the community and economy in ways the church rarely measures. Consider these concrete realities:

- Scotty's Automotive helps feed, clothe, and house 40-plus people because he employs six other mechanics. Each of these families participates in the community and economy: working, spending, and giving of their time to serve others.

- Hundreds of people bring their cars to Scotty's shop each month. They come in crisis, needing help in order to tend to their daily affairs. His successful repairs enable folks to offer thousands of productive hours of work that would be lost if their cars remained unrepaired or required frequent returns. Beyond just work, Scotty enables families to take vacations safely, get to church and sporting events, and carry out charitable and cultural activities because their cars are sound.

- Scotty says that he and his team possess about the same volume of knowledge as a general physician. With computers, changing technology, and ongoing training, the day of the "shade-tree mechanic" has essentially passed.

- Let's go further. Scotty pays his taxes, thus contributing (with some grumbling about how the money is spent) to the social good. He pays into workers' compensation and health care benefits, directly and indirectly supporting the medical community. The rent he pays for his large building space provides income for the landlord that eventually finds its way back into the economy.

The ripple effect of one family business represents much more than a job that allows a couple to tithe and pay their bills. Scotty and his team are connected with millions of dollars in the local economy, and their efforts contribute to a flourishing community. In the midst of all this, they have led many to Christ, strengthened the faith of others, and offered a sterling witness to neighbors who aren't involved in the church. Scotty has quietly helped several struggling families with reduced-cost repairs. He makes sure his customers are safe, and he never does work unless it is needed.

Why is Scotty's story important? Because it touches on every major theme in this book. Making disciples is the content of the Great Commission. Godly character, healthy relationships, and vocational clarity are vital for every believer, every local church, and the larger body of Christ to fulfill their purpose. Spiritual leaders are dedicated to seeing church members grow as they reach out to their community and glorify Christ by allowing the Holy Spirit to use them.

The missing piece in our discipleship is the integration of faith, work, and economics so that Christians are not only ethical and excellent at work but see their work as part of God's larger design for their community, state, and nation to flourish! This work is designed to correct this gap and empower Spirit-filled leaders with tools to equip local churches as powerful places of the presence of God and as communities that commission members to see their work as worship and the flourishing of the community as part of the Great Commission. Each person's daily work is their ministry before God and a watching world.

As Pentecostal believers, we are urgent about the Great Commission (Matthew 28:18–20; Acts 1:8) and rely on the power of the Holy Spirit to go across the street and around the world. We expect supernatural signs to confirm the preaching of the gospel, and we affirm that all believers – regardless of age, class, ethnicity, or gender – can be empowered by the Spirit to fulfill the mission of God as we prepare for the soon return of Christ.

As we go into the world, we are led by the Spirit to create charities, dig wells, offer medical help, develop educational institutions, care for the outcasts, and even start businesses to provide resources or open doors in "closed" situations. All these efforts need to continue and grow.

As Martin Luther's great hymn, "A Mighty Fortress Is Our God," declares in the last verse, "The Spirit and the gifts are ours." Pentecostals now number in the tens of millions in the United States and in the hundreds of millions around the world, encompassing all cultures and permeating all Christian traditions. Our movement, though now a century old, shows no signs of slowing; and for this we must thank God for his sovereign grace and merciful outpourings.

The passion and urgency of mission must be joined with the panorama of the purpose of God so that we completely fulfill the plan of God in our day. Spirit-filled Christianity touches all of life. Living in the power of the Holy Spirit includes active participation in the economy, work as worship, and "providential increases" (John Wesley) in the influence of the kingdom of God.

Scotty's story is repeated many times over by faithful followers of Christ. Our aim is to help believers become aware of and energized by the connection between their faith and work, and between their personal and social influence.

Scotty's story is part of a larger divine drama that is God's eternal purpose to glorify himself in the story of his relationship with humankind. God's story is majestic and mysterious, boundless yet occurring in real places and through real people. When our stories align with the Lord's, something beautiful happens: God's people become the source of his "manifold" (colorful, many-splendored) wisdom on display to the universe (Ephesians. 3:10).

REFLECTION QUESTIONS

1. What impressed you the most about Scotty's story? What questions does it raise in your mind?

2. How do most people in your church view their daily work, whether in business, at home, at school, or as volunteers?

3. Where do you see the "ripple effect" of the work done by those in your church?

4. How do you measure spiritual growth?

Made for
WORK

Amy Sherman

Because we are made for full-time discipleship that serves God and neighbor, we are made to work – in the home, in the workplace, in schools, in neighborhoods. We are made to flourish in community, with each of us making our own contribution to the flourishing of all. That's why work takes up most of life! In this wise and theologically rich essay, Amy Sherman unfolds the Kingdom significance of our daily work. She shows that doing good work is central to the kingdom of God, and the Kingdom is central to doing good work.

Amy Sherman is a senior fellow and the director of the Center on Faith in Communities at the Sagamore Institute. She also serves on the advisory board of the Christian Community Development Association and is a senior fellow at International Justice Mission. She lives in Charlottesville, Va., where she founded Charlottesville Abundant Life Ministries. She has a Ph.D. in economic development and works with churches, anti-poverty organizations, and other nonprofits to help them minister more effectively. She is also a leader in the Acton Institute's Vocation Infusion Learning Community, which helps churches put vocation at the center of church life. If you like this essay, check out her book, "Kingdom Calling," which shows how work is an opportunity to advance God's kingdom and provides practical advice for churches to help make this central to Christian living. Her other books include "Preferential Option," "Restorers of Hope," "Reinvigorating Faith in Communities," and "The Soul of Development."

Introduction: God's Gracious Invitation to Join Him in His Work

God is at work in the world, and he has called us to join him in that work. This is a wondrous truth: we marvel that the all-powerful, all-knowing, all-sufficient, and perfectly holy God would desire to use *us*, his fallen and frail creatures, in his work. Yet it is true, and it is seen repeatedly throughout the Scriptures.

The invitation is extended right at the beginning. God creates paradise, but it is incomplete because there is "no one to work the ground" (Genesis 2:5) until he fashions human beings in his own image. These image-bearers are then given what we might call the Great Mandate: to work and take care of the Garden (Genesis 2:16) and to fill it and rule over it (Genesis 1:28). In this – and in the seven-fold repetition, "God saw it was good" – we see God's delight in his creation and his affirmation of this physical world. As Andy Crouch helpfully notes in "Culture Making," the biblical story shows God calling human beings not only into a spiritual task of worshipping him, but also into a cultural task.[21] God doesn't divide the world into sacred and secular, affirming only the former. God is at work sustaining and providing for his creation, and he accomplishes much of that work through human hands. Christian truck drivers, farmers, engineers, and grocery store clerks are engaged in godly work just as pastors and missionaries are through their vocations. There are no "second-class citizens" in the church.

The invitation to join God in his work in the world continues in what we might label the Great Call in Genesis 12:1-3. At this point in the Great Narrative of Scripture, the world has collapsed into ruin as a result of the Fall. But God has a magnificent plan for redemption and restoration. He is on a mission, as theologian Christopher Wright says, to bring blessing to the world and "put everything to rights."[22] This *missio Dei* is the sending love of God poured into the world to bring about restoration of all that was lost in the Fall: peace with God, peace with self, peace with others, and peace with creation. And God decides to use a human family, Abraham's, as a vehicle through which he will work. In Genesis 12, God promises to bless Abraham and make him a blessing to all the peoples on the earth.

In the Old Testament, this "being-a-blessing" involved a worshipful relationship with God expressed through personal and corporate lives, totally God-shaped, marked by all sorts of special laws and practices meant to distinguish as holy Abraham's family, distinct from the rest of the world's cultures. The prophet Micah offers a shorthand description of this holy, being-a-blessing lifestyle in the words

---

[21] Andy Crouch, "Culture Making: Recovering Our Creative Calling" (Downers Grove: InterVarsity Press, 2008), 256.

[22] Christopher Wright, "The Mission of God's People: A Biblical Theology of the Church's Mission," ed. Jonathan Lunde (Grand Rapids: Zondervan, 2010), 284.

of what we might call the Great Requirement in Micah 6:8: "He has shown you, O Man, what is good. And what does the LORD require of you but to do justice, love kindness, and to walk humbly with your God?" God's followers were called to a whole-life discipleship, to a relationship with God through which they would offer worship through everything they did, everything they said, and everything they were (Deuteronomy 6:5; Leviticus 11:45; Proverbs 3:6).

The Israelites, God's chosen community of Abraham's descendants, largely failed in their work to be a blessing. Rather than shining as a light that drew attention to the beauty of the loving, holy, One True God, the Israelites too often simply blended in with the cultures and nations around them, imitating their idolatry and injustice.

But God's plan of salvation was not dependent on human Israel. From the very beginning (Genesis 3:15) he promised one special descendent from Israel's line who would be the Great Servant (Isaiah 53) of his will to accomplish his purposes. Jesus, the God-Man, was this Servant. Jesus gave his life as atonement for sin, destroying both its guilt and corruption, and fully satisfying the justice of God. God raised him from the dead and crowned him as King with all authority. King Jesus now reigns from heaven, reconciling to himself "all things" (Colossians 1:15-20).

Jesus' Ministry ... And Ours

The ultimate goal of the *missio Dei* is the full realization of the kingdom of God. As Dutch theologian Johannes Verkuyl writes: "[I]n both the Old Testament and New, God by both his words and deeds claims that he is intent on bringing the kingdom of God to expression and restoring his liberating domain of authority."[23] Not surprisingly, Jesus uses the phrases "the kingdom of God" and "the kingdom of heaven" numerous times during his earthly ministry. In the Sermon of the Mount, the great monologue about life in this Kingdom, Jesus summarizes its being-a-blessing character. This is because the church, Abraham's spiritual descendants through faith in Christ's righteousness, share in the Great Call to be a blessing. This is what Kingdom citizenship is about. And "Kingdom citizens" are what we are when we accept Jesus' offer of salvation. His evangelistic invitation is "enter" (or "receive") the kingdom of God (Matthew 5:20; Matthew 21:31; Matthew 25:34; John 3:3; Luke 18:17).

Through the ministry of his Son, God renews the invitation for humans to join in the *missio Dei*. As Dean Flemming puts it in "Recovering the Full Mission of God," "Jesus of Nazareth gives God's loving mission a face, a voice, a pair of

---

[23] Johannes Verkuyl, "The Kingdom of God as the Goal of the Missio Dei," International Review of Mission 68, no. 270: (April 1979), doi: 10.1111/j.1758-6631.1979.tb01307.x.

sandals."[24] Jesus announces, embodies, and enacts the Good News of the kingdom of God. This seamless, three-fold "being-telling-doing" of Jesus' ministry sets the model for our own. Obviously, a major part of Jesus' mission was unique to him personally as the Son of God and Savior of the world. We can never do the propitiating work of redemption that he did, nor are we called or expected to. Nonetheless, Jesus does invite us into his restorative work. He calls us to follow him, and defines that as involving love *for* him and work *with* him according to his purposes. Consider, for example, Jesus' reinstatement of Peter in John 21:15-17. Peter is given the opportunity both to affirm his love for Jesus and to accept his assignment from Jesus ("feed my sheep").

The nature of Jesus' invitation to join him in his work is also seen clearly in Mark 3:13-15. There we read:

> Jesus went up on a mountainside and called to him those he wanted, and they came to him. He appointed twelve that they might be with him and that he might send them out to preach and to have authority to drive out demons.

As Flemming points out, this call incorporates the being-telling-doing activities of Jesus himself. The call is to *be* with Jesus, to *tell* (preach) the gospel, and to *do* the works of healing and evil-destroying that Jesus was doing.[25] Luke offers similar descriptions of the commissioning of Jesus' followers (see Luke 9:1-6; Luke 10). Jesus' invitation for his disciples to join him in his work is seen in the book of John as well. There, Jesus speaks frequently of his identity as the "sent one" and then tells his flock, "As the Father has sent Me, so I am sending you" (John 20:21; see also John 17:18).

So we can say it again: God (Father, Son, and Holy Spirit) is at work in the world, and he has invited us to join him. Being his disciple means following him joyfully in that work. And that has numerous implications for our daily work.

Our Work and the Being-Telling-Doing of the Kingdom

As disciples of Christ, we imitate him in his work. As noted earlier, his work involved announcing the gospel of the Kingdom, embodying that Kingdom, and enacting/demonstrating that Kingdom. This provides a helpful structure for gaining an understanding of how to be Christ's disciples in and through our daily work. We can examine more deeply each of these three dimensions in the life of Jesus and discover life lessons as his disciples in our workplaces.

---

[24] Dean Flemming, "Recovering the Full Mission of God: A Biblical Perspective on Being, Doing and Telling" (Downers Grove: InterVarsity Press, 2013), 61.

[25] Ibid., 80.

Being

Jesus *embodied* the kingdom of God.

Scholar Lucien Legrand wrote: "The Gospel was not only proclaimed by Jesus: that Gospel was transparent [in] all His work."[26] Jesus was message and messenger. He was the "Word made flesh" (John 1:14). He embodied the reign of God that he announced.[27]

As his followers, Jesus calls us to be with him and become like him. Before Jesus calls us to do things *for* him, he invites us to come and be *with* him. He breathes his own Spirit *into* us. There is an interior reality to the kingdom of God; it involves something new happening in us (as we become new creatures in Christ). Our whole being comes under the lordship of King Jesus; we gladly say "yes" to the reign of God, and welcome it as the path of true life. The Spirit in us works faithfully to conform us to the image of Jesus. We imitate Jesus' embodiment of the kingdom of God when our character grows to be more like his; when we imitate his servant nature; and when our personal and communal life bears witness to his winsome and beautiful holiness – to the reality that life in the Kingdom is indeed the abundant life.

All this has direct relevance to us as workers. We are to "adorn" our profession of the gospel by being certain kinds of people. For example, we witness to the reality of God's reign when we:

- Are people of Spirit-dependent peace and self-control in the midst of stressful and frenetic work environments;
- Are Spirit-empowered team players and servants in work cultures where cutthroat competition is the norm;
- Are Spirit-formed, humble, kind, gracious, and patient people with our employers, co-workers, and clients; and
- Live out our identity as God's loved children, not basing our self-worth on our job status or performance, nor making work an idol.

Embodying the Kingdom in our daily work will also involve our intentional reliance on Jesus. Our Lord tells us plainly in John 15:5 that apart from him we can do nothing. But if we remain in the vine (which is Christ), we will bear much fruit. "Remaining" and "abiding" in the vine involve cultivating and practicing the presence of Christ, being with him, and asking him to empower us for each

---

[26] Lucien Legrand, "Unity and Plurality: Mission in the Bible" (London: SCM Press, 1965), 65.
[27] Flemming, 71.

task before us – even those we might feel confident we can do in our own natural strength or giftedness.

Telling

Jesus *announced* the kingdom of God.

He preached and proclaimed it. Matthew 4:17 and Mark 1:14 use the Greek word *kerysso* for Jesus' "proclaiming" the reign of God. Luke uses *kerysso* when recounting Jesus' inaugural address in Luke 4 when the Messiah quotes Isaiah 61 on "proclaiming" freedom for the prisoners.[28] Matthew 9:35 and Luke 8:1 tell of Jesus "proclaiming" the Good News of the Kingdom throughout cities and villages.

The gospel is news, and as D.A. Carson emphasized, news is meant to be announced.[29] While evangelism is more than mere words (more on that later), it is incomplete without words. Jesus "proclaimed" (*kerysso*) and "taught" (Greek *didasko*) the gospel of the Kingdom. *Didasko* is used 55 times in the four gospels. Jesus preached the gospel using words.

The content of this Good News surely deserves proclamation from every rooftop; it is the announcement of the dawning of God's kingdom, breaking into the world in dramatic fashion in the person of Christ. Faithful Jews had been longing for this Kingdom – the future reality prophetically described in "preview passages"[30] such as Isaiah 65, Ezekiel 34, and Psalm 72 – when all that was lost in the Fall would be restored. Jesus' announcement is that in him, nothing less than *shalom* – the way to restored peace with God, peace with self, peace with others, and peace with the creation – has drawn near.

Jesus' central preaching topic was the kingdom of God. His speech and his Kingdom ways often confounded his hearers, though, because his teaching did not always align with their preconceived notions. For example, Jesus taught that the Kingdom is both now and not yet. He announced that it has drawn near (Mark 1:14-15) and is "in their midst" (Luke 17:21). Yet he also speaks of it as a coming, future reality (Matthew 26:29) and instructs his followers to pray for its consummation ("Your Kingdom come, your will be done, on earth as it is

---

[28] Walter A. Elwell, "Preach, Proclaim," Evangelical Dictionary of Theology, 2014, http://www.biblestudytools.com/dictionaries/bakers-evangelical-dictionary/preach-proclaim.html.

[29] D. A. Carson, "What is the Gospel?–Revisited," in "For the Fame of God's Name: Essays in Honor of John Piper," ed. Sam Storms and Justin Taylor (Wheaton: Crossway Books, 2010), 158.

[30] The phrase is Rev. Jeff White's (pastor of New Song Harlem in New York City). By it he means those biblical texts that offer glimpses into what life in the fully consummated heaven and earth will be like. Additional preview passages include Zechariah 8, Isaiah 32, Micah 4, Amos 9, and Revelations 21 and 22.

in heaven"). As Article 24 of the Mennonite Confession of Faith puts it, "Jesus proclaimed the nearness of God's reign and its future realization."[31]

Many were also confounded by Jesus' redefinition of Kingdom membership. Jesus preached (and lived) an inclusive gospel. Although his own ministry was primarily to "the lost sheep of Israel," Jesus also talked to Samaritans (John 4) and taught in the Decapolis – 10 largely pagan cities to the east of the Sea of Galilee (see Mark 7:31ff). He dined and conversed with "sinners and tax collectors," much to the disgust of the Pharisees (Luke 15:1-2). Those who thought the Kingdom was solely for the Jews (and then only for those Jews who practiced the fullness of the Law) were indignant at Jesus' outreach, even though his interpretation of the Kingdom was more biblical. After all, the initial promise that God made to Abraham was that through him *all* nations would be blessed. Moreover, many of the Old Testament preview passages speak of the pagan nations and their kings coming to worship in the New Jerusalem (Isaiah 11:5-10; Isaiah 56: 1-8; Isaiah 60; Zechariah 8:23). The Old Testament's teaching is not only that the Kingdom is indeed going to be restored to the Jews one day – but also that it will be extended to Gentiles.

The "telling" of Jesus not only involved confounding speech, but also confrontational speech. The gospel is indeed Good News, but it is demanding news as well. It urgently calls for a whole-hearted response of repentance. It requires surrendering all other pursuits and the kingdom of self and turning oneself wholly to God. Additionally, it is offensive to many post-moderns because it claims to be *the* one True Story. Proclaiming the gospel also offends because it contends that *Jesus*, alone, is Lord, which means that many other things with claims to lordship (race, culture, national identity, Caesar, Mammon, empire, class) are *not* Lord. And as Lord, Jesus has authority to make judgments about what is and is not just.

Jesus was unafraid to oppose what stood in the way of *shalom*, whether it was political, religious, cultural, spiritual, or economic power. By his words, he cast out demons (Luke 4:33-36; Mark 5:1-20; Mark 9:20ff) and freed people from illnesses described as spiritual oppressions (for example, Luke 13:10-12). By his word, he controlled and manipulated the physical universe (as in the changing of water into wine in John 2:6-9) and commanded the wind and waves (Matthew 8:23-27). He confronted cultural mores by fellowshipping with prostitutes and including women among his close friends – permitting Mary, for example, to "sit at his feet" as he taught (Luke 10:38-39). He denounced religious and economic oppression by the scribes and Pharisees in a lengthy monologue (Matthew 23).

---

[31] Article 24, "The Reign of God," Mennonite Confession of Faith, 1995, http://www.mennolink.org/doc/cof/art.24.html.

He chastised exploitative businesspeople who took advantage of the poor in the temple markets (Matthew 21:12-13), indicting them for turning God's house of prayer into "a den of robbers."

Once again, this has practical implications for our day-to-day work lives. First, relationships at work offer opportunities to share the story of Jesus. Christian business owners can hire company chaplains to provide pastoral ministry in the workplace. Christian employees can seek to establish workplace Bible studies and invite non-believers. They can pray for their colleagues. They can listen carefully to the struggles faced by their coworkers, and talk about the hope, peace, joy, and help they have received from our loving heavenly Father. The sad fact that Christians often conduct such evangelism poorly, failing to be winsome and sensitive, doesn't change the reality that being a Kingdom citizen involves telling others about that Kingdom and its King.

Second, Jesus' teaching on the now-and-not-yet-ness of the Kingdom provides us with a realistic perspective on our daily work. On the one hand, we should be filled with optimism, recognizing that the in-breaking of the Kingdom means that Jesus has already begun the work of "renewing all things" (Matthew 19:28). We can expect him to transform us into more Christ-like workers, and to use us, our speech, our witness, and our work in ways that bring about positive changes in our organizations. On the other hand, the not-yet-ness of the Kingdom protects us from utopianism, expecting that in this life, our work will no longer be "toil." Until Jesus returns, we continue to labor in a fallen world, among fallen sinners like ourselves, and our work will sometimes be futile or frustrating.

Third, Jesus' model of "telling" suggests we may want to add some additional aspects to the traditional notion of "workplace evangelism." Just as Jesus sought fellowship with those at the margins, we can pursue inclusive hospitality at our workplaces. This might look like deliberately pursuing friendships with coworkers from different ethnic, cultural, or religious backgrounds – or with employees occupying the lowest rungs of the firm (e.g., janitors), who may often feel invisible. It might mean creating opportunities for low-income or minority youth who are largely unfamiliar with our industry to come onsite for job shadowing days or short internships. And just as Jesus engaged in confrontational speech, our "workplace evangelism" may at times mean boldly speaking the truth to power. It may look like being a whistleblower who speaks out about abuses or fraud in the company. Or it may involve working with a team to articulate a set of operating principles or standards that "raises the bar" of industry practice. James Davison Hunter spoke about this notion of confrontation beautifully in his important book, "To Change the World:"

> The church, as it exists within the wide range of individual vocations in every sphere of social life (commerce, philanthropy, education, etc.) must

be present in the world in ways that work toward the *constructive* subversion of all frameworks of social life that are incompatible with the shalom for which we were made and to which we are called. As a natural expression of its passion to honor God in all things and to love our neighbor as ourselves, the church and its people will challenge all structures that dishonor God, dehumanize people, and neglect or do harm to the creation.[32]

Doing

Jesus *enacted* the kingdom of God.

Jesus' ministry combined words and deeds. We see him feeding and healing people, responding to their needs. He interpreted his works in Kingdom language. When he cast out a demon from a suffering man in Luke 11, and the Pharisees protested that Jesus worked such miracles through Beelzebub's power, Jesus responded, "If I cast out demons by the finger of God *then the Kingdom of God has come upon you.*" Jesus' miracles were signs and demonstrations that the Kingdom had – as he said – arrived in him. When John the Baptist sent messengers to Jesus to try to confirm whether Jesus was truly the Messiah, Jesus pointed to his actions as the validation. "Go back and report to John what you have seen and heard," replied Jesus. "The blind receive sight, the lame walk, those who have leprosy are cleansed, the deaf hear, the dead are raised, and the good news is proclaimed to the poor" (Luke 7:22). This is the Good News in action.

These deeds capture the eschatological hope of the New Heavens and New Earth (that is, the fully realized kingdom of God) prophesied in the Old Testament preview passages. Consider Jesus' reply in Luke 7:22 in light of, for example, Isaiah's vision of the restoration God would one day bring:

> In that day the eyes of the blind shall be opened,
> and the ears of the deaf unstopped;
> then the lame shall leap like a deer,
> and the tongue of the speechless sing for joy (Isaiah 35:5-6).

This is why we can speak of Jesus' ministry as one of bringing foretastes of the future Kingdom into present reality. And this provides a wonderful framework for thinking about how we can steward our vocational power well; that is, our skills, knowledge, networks, platform, position, and reputation. Just as Jesus brought foretastes of the Kingdom, we can deploy our vocational power to advance such foretastes.

---

[32] James Davison Hunter, "To Change the World: The Irony, Tragedy, & Possibility of Christianity in the Late Modern World" (New York: Oxford University Press, 2010), 235. Emphasis in the original.

Table 1 illustrates the marks of the consummated Kingdom under the four categories of *shalom* mentioned earlier (peace with God, self, others, and creation).

Table 1. Marks of the Consummated Kingdom

Peace with God Intimacy with God Beauty Joy	**Peace with Self** Health/Wholeness Hope Comfort
Peace with Others Unity/Community Security Lack of Violence Reconciliation Justice	**Peace with the Creation** Economic Flourishing Sustainability

One fruitful avenue of faith/work integration is to consider which of these particular Kingdom foretastes our individual professions might be well-suited to advance. Some of this comes rather easily; medical personnel have opportunities to advance wholeness, business entrepreneurs have opportunities to promote economic flourishing, and artists have opportunities to promote beauty. Sometimes the exercise might be a bit more challenging.[33] Either way, it helps us to think about living the Kingdom through work itself. We have spoken already in this essay about the *kind of workers* we should aspire to be in light of our Kingdom citizenship. We've said that we should be workers who display the character of Jesus, workers who abide in Jesus and draw upon his strength for fulfilling our labors, and workers who speak words of truth about Jesus and his kingdom – words both comforting and invitational, as well as prophetic and confrontational. But living out our faith "on the job" is not only about the kinds of workers we are or the kinds of relationships we pursue at work. It is also about the work itself. The work itself matters.

We can gain some insight by reflecting on how life in the Kingdom involves obedience to both the Great Commandment, to love God and neighbor (Matthew 22:35-40), and to the Great Commission, to "go into the all the world and make disciples" (Matthew 28:18-20). Both can, and should, shape our work lives. Pastors need to see this, so that their call to discipleship includes not just "private" discipleship (in our personal lives of family, friends, and church), but "public"

---

[33] How, for example, does a comedian, a professional football player, or a paper chemist advance Kingdom foretastes? For some stories, see my book, "Kingdom Calling: Vocational Stewardship for the Common Good" (Downers Grove: InterVarsity Press, 2011).

discipleship (living out our faith in the marketplace). Jesus certainly understood this, setting 45 out of his 52 parables in the marketplace.[34]

To enact the Great Commandment through our work is to offer that work up as worship to God, and to love and serve our neighbors through it. Even menial or tedious work can be done in a way that reveals obedience to the Great Commandment. The certified nursing assistant at the hospital who changes sheets and bedpans is offering essential, practical, humble service to the sick and their loved ones. Her work is practical love in action. The store clerk, who listens attentively, responds proactively, goes the extra mile to resolve a dilemma, and cheerfully offers advice when asked, serves his customers well. A factory worker may have little interaction with the customer of the product she helps make. But that product – whether a tire, a toy, a table, or a truck – contributes to meeting human needs. Her work matters, and it glorifies God and serves neighbors when it is done with excellence and diligence that helps ensure the quality and reliability of the product.

Everyone who is doing good, honest work should take deep satisfaction from their labor. They are extending the influence of God's *shalom* into the world, and by doing so, enacting the kingdom of God. This may be obvious for those fortunate enough to work for firms that create products that have dramatic, positive influence on human flourishing – think of a new medicine that cures a disease, or an irrigation system that boosts productivity for farmers, or an improved kind of protective gear for firemen. But those creating the ordinary goods and services that people rely on every day – from diapers to pavement to elevators, and a million other things – contribute to human flourishing, too.

In "To Change the World," Hunter draws our attention to a broader understanding of the Great Commission and how it connects to our vocations. While Jesus' closing words in Matthew 28 are usually interpreted in *geographic* terms – go into all the world, meaning the nations of the world – they can legitimately be understood in *sociological* terms as well.[35] That is, "go into all the world" can mean enter all the sectors of society – finance, art, politics, education, law, commerce, diplomacy, healthcare, engineering, architecture, and so forth – and work to advance the Kingdom there.

We enact the Great Commission when we penetrate all the different sectors of society for *shalom's* purposes, operating according to the biblical truth that Christ's Lordship pervades "every square inch" of this world (in the well-known

---

[34] Stevens, "Work Matters" (See Introduction).
[35] Hunter, "To Change the World," 257.

phrase of Abraham Kuyper). We labor in these spheres to see the ramifications of God's reign begin to take hold, not only in individual life, but in institutional life. Social structures cannot be "discipled" in the same way that people are. But through our work, we can introduce reforms into social structures that nudge "the way things are done around here" from is, to ought.

What does that look like? Perhaps we find ourselves in a system that is supposed to deliver quality health care to the elderly, but is not doing so due to inefficiencies. So we work to change the world as it is to what it ought be, causing improvements in service delivery. Or perhaps we find ourselves in a system that, through a series of informal norms and the traditions of organizational culture, effectively stymies the advancement of female professionals beyond a certain glass ceiling. So we labor to correct this injustice. Or perhaps we find ourselves in a school system that is failing its low-income students, and so we work to implement curricular reforms to spark student engagement. In all these activities, we are laboring in small ways for "the renewal of all things" promised by our King Jesus. We are caring about the things that Jesus cares about: justice, wholeness, opportunity, flourishing, beauty, hope, and reconciliation. We are working, through our work, to bring greater foretastes of these Kingdom realities into existence. We are working to put processes and products in line with God's vision.

Summing Up

The scope of God's work in the world is amazing and vast. He continues to actively shepherd his creation, providing for and sustaining it (Psalms 65:9-13; Psalms 104:10-14; Psalms 145). He is also active in the world, restraining evil through his common grace.[36] And he is busy in the work of renewing all things toward the end of redemptive history – the consummation of his Kingdom, wherein there will be no more sin, evil, suffering, pain, or death. When Christ returns, the New Jerusalem will "come down from heaven as a bride beautifully prepared for her husband" (Revelations 21:2) and the invisible reign of God will become the visible realm of God.

We are already citizens of that realm. Our entry into that "better country" (Hebrews 11:16) has been secured by the gracious death and resurrection of King Jesus. We live now as dual citizens – of this world and the world to come – and have opportunities to be ambassadors of the Kingdom of Light. Just as God sent Jesus to us, Jesus sends us into our vocations to announce, embody, and enact the Good News. Though in this still-broken world our work sometimes feels insignificant, our daily labors are in fact high callings. Through them, we

---

[36] Dr. S. Lewis Johnson puts it this way: "Common grace curbs sin, it maintains moral order in the universe, it distributes gifts and talents among men." See "The Doctrine of Common Grace," SLJ Institute, 2014, http://sljinstitute.net/systematic-theology/soteriology/the-doctrine-of-common-grace/.

have opportunities to reflect God in the ways he works: God-as-Provider, God-as-Restrainer, God-as-Restorer. Relying on Jesus' own Spirit, we can creatively and strategically advance foretastes of the consummated Kingdom through the deployment of our vocational skills and expertise. The abundant life Jesus invites us into is one of finding deep meaning and purpose, both by being *with* him and by *joining* him in his Kingdom-advancing work through our own daily labors.

REFLECTION QUESTIONS

1. How important is work in the original creation design of humanity? How important is work in the redemptive *missio Dei* into which Christ sends his followers?

2. What is the purpose of work? What does Sherman mean by "being-a-blessing"?

3. Consider the items listed on Table 1, "Marks of the Consummated Kingdom." How many of these is your church actively equipping Christians to pursue?

Made for
HOPE

Greg Forster

The world of work is broken, painful, toilsome, and frustrating. We are made for work, but in this fallen world we must do that work under conditions we were definitely *not* made for. The central, daily challenge of Christian life for millions of believers is discovering the presence of God in broken work – finding the meaning, dignity, and spiritual satisfaction of working to serve God and neighbor in the midst of toil and trial. In this heartfelt essay on Lester DeKoster's book "Work: The Meaning of Your Life," Greg Forster explains why a sound theology of work must include a theology of suffering and culminate in a message of hope that speaks to all workers.

Greg Forster is a program director in the Faith, Work, and Economics program at The Kern Family Foundation in Waukesha, Wis. He holds a Ph.D. with distinction in political science from Yale University. If you like this essay, check out his most recent book, "Joy for the World," with a foreword by Tim Keller; the book describes how Christianity lost its influence in American culture and how the church can begin rebuilding it. Forster is also a senior fellow at the Friedman Foundation for Educational Choice and the editor of the group blog, Hang Together. His other books include "The Joy of Calvinism," "Starting with Locke," "The Contested Public Square," "Education Myths," and "John Locke's Politics of Moral Consensus." He contributes regularly to The Gospel Coalition, First Thoughts, and other online outlets.

One day, two things dawned on me:

1. If life is to have meaning, I would have to find it, not hope to create it for myself.

2. Living must get its meaning, first of all, on the job, because that's the drain down ... which the best hours of each week dribble away.

At first, these options seemed fanciful: Life's meaning on the job? Not because I put it there, but because work endows living with significance? Kidding somebody?

No kidding at all. That's the way it is.

"Work: The Meaning of Your Life: A Christian Perspective" (xiv).

· · · · · · · ·

When they first hear the message of the faith and work movement, a lot of people roll their eyes. *Made for work?* they think. *That's a nice theory. You should try doing my job.*

This is a deep problem for the faith and work movement. A recent Gallup survey found that 70 percent of American workers feel disengaged at work or outright hate their jobs.[37] That's on top of 10 million Americans who want to work but are unemployed and the steadily increasing number of people – now fully 30 percent of adult men – who aren't even looking for work.[38] Our culture isn't always well prepared for the message that work is a great and glorious thing.

The world of work is also changing rapidly. New technologies and the global economy continue to reshape who does what, how they do it, what they get paid for it, and just about every other structural aspect of our work. Because we know that the world of work is broken, the rapid pace of change can be frightening. Where can we turn for security? Is there a moral order in our work that does not change, even though all of its conditions seem to be subject to almost limitless innovation? Will technological advances and global competition dehumanize us, reducing the worker to just another cog in the machine?

In this essay, we will look at how one author dealt with these problems by putting the Christian virtue of hope front and center. Lester DeKoster wrote his profound

---

[37] "State of the American Workplace," Gallup Inc., June 2013, http://www.gallup.com/strategicconsulting/163007/state-american-workplace.aspx.

[38] "The Employment Situation – May 2014," U.S. Bureau of Labor Statistics, June 2014, http://www.bls.gov/news.release/archives/empsit_06062014.pdf; Nicholas Eberstadt, "The Astonishing Collapse of Work in America," Real Clear Markets, July 2013, http://www.realclearmarkets.com/articles/2013/07/10/the_astonishing_collapse_of_work_in_america_100465.html.

little book "Work: The Meaning of Your Life" for factory workers who felt utterly degraded and demoralized by their labor. His message of hope to them is an outstanding model for our movement today. And his deep thinking about work points us away from superficial approaches and toward a three-dimensional model of what it means to work.

Does Good Really Run Deeper Than Evil?

Work is broken for all of us, because we and our world are broken. We feel that brokenness in our work every day. It's toilsome. It's frustrating. A lot of the time, we feel more like the work is doing us than we are doing it. On top of that, coworkers can be hostile, manipulative, even dishonest. And if we do everything right, all our hard work can still fall apart and come to nothing due to forces outside our control.

Theologically, it is critical to keep our affirmation of the goodness of work front and center. God's activity in creation and redemption must always be seen as more powerful and more important – more *ultimate* – than our brokenness and the brokenness of our world. Good runs deeper than evil in this universe, and talking as though evil runs just as deep as good is not just a mistake. It is damnable heresy.

And yet, paradoxically, if we start with God's goodness and how we can find it in our work, many people struggle to connect that to their daily experience in any tangible way. There are some who can do so, by God's grace. But many find little connection between the theoretical affirmation of God's goodness and their practical experience of toil and frustration – of the enormity of evil and the curse, dragging us down day after day.

Thus we seem to be caught in a trap. If we talk about work as a place of goodness and light, where God is present and active, for many this seems disconnected from their daily reality. But if we talk about work as a place of darkness and curse, we risk losing the gospel itself. For the gospel says that God really is, in fact, the only ultimate ruler of this universe, and he really has, in fact, defeated evil and swallowed up the darkness in his glorious light.

Hope is the key that opens this lock. It is the only sword that can cut this Gordian knot. With our eyes, we often see a world dominated by evil and curse. But we are to live by faith, not by sight (2 Corinthians 5:7). And what is this faith that is so powerful that we can live by it, even in defiance of our own sight? It is the assurance of what we hope for (Hebrews 11:1).

The art of helping people live out their faith in their work is largely the art of *giving them something to hope for*. It is the art of helping them become aware of the larger realities that define the deepest meaning of their work. Their eyes don't see these larger realities on a daily basis; our job is to help them remember these things when their eyes don't see them.

Crucially, the "larger realities" people need to remember include more than just the spiritual realities that eyes can never see. They also include a lot of plain, humdrum facts in the material world that we don't see every day, simply because we don't happen to bump into them. In their work, people must not only know Christ (who is not seen because he is present through the Spirit). They must also know the millions of neighbors their work is serving (who are not seen because they are physically remote from the workplace). It is this broader sight, both of spiritual realities and of material realities that are physically remote, that makes hope possible.

This brings us to Lester DeKoster and his powerful little book.

Only Hopeful Work Can Build a Meaningful Life

DeKoster, a professor at Calvin College, gave speech classes in the evenings for blue-collar workers in his city. He heard most of them describe their daily lives at work as meaningless and degrading. They felt like they were nobodies, like they were slaves, like they were just part of the machinery on the shop floor, like no one cared about them as human beings. They saw no dignity or meaning in what they did.

DeKoster knew that this darkness, large as it might loom in their sight, was not the deepest truth about their work. So in 1982, he wrote them – and all other workers who labor in the darkness – a book: "Work: The Meaning of Your Life."

Interpreting their experiences in the light of the parables of Matthew 25, DeKoster laid out a simple but powerful framework for connecting work to both gospel hope and the structures of human civilization. At 62 pages, it is a beautiful gift that continues to give to the church today.

DeKoster argues that we must bring hope to our work if we are to have hope at all. Our view of work shapes our lives more than anything else, simply because we spend more time working than doing anything else. Work is not all of life, but it is central to how we find meaning, purpose, and dignity in our existence – or fail to find it.

Those who don't find transcendent meaning in their work live as though their existence is mostly meaningless. Their character and life choices are shaped accordingly. Even if they are Christians, if they don't connect their faith to their work, they will be what Doug Spada and Dave Scott call "Monday Morning Atheists," living the bulk of their lives *as though* they are without God and without hope in the world. Their faith, while real, remains confined within the bounds of what Mark Greene calls "leisure-time Christianity."

DeKoster writes that for people who don't find meaning in work, whether Christian or not, human life is essentially "a wilderness of work." Each day is a desert of meaningless toil that we have to trudge through, day after day. Our burning thirst for significance is quenched only occasionally – and briefly – by the "oases of meaning furnished by our families, the church, politics, community affairs, plus hobbies and spectator sports thrown in to give zest to leisure." (xiii)

The remedy to this bleak existence, DeKoster argues, comes when "a right view of work becomes the key to a satisfying life." If we live out a God-centered approach to work, we will be grounding the bulk of our lives squarely in God. Our spiritual longings will be satisfied.

Moreover, DeKoster boldly asserts that "if work can give a central core of meaning to living, then all other meanings cluster around this one." (xv) Though we might yearn for a different kind of life – one in which work is peripheral – that's just not the way we're wired. God has *designed* us to spend most of our lives working.

So for DeKoster, bringing hope to the world of work is not only crucial to finding meaning in our work, but to finding meaning in our lives as a whole. If we do our daily work without the hope that God is present and active in it, our lives become "a wilderness of work," a desert through which we trudge, desperately thirsting for meaning and purpose. If we work with hope, that thirst will be satisfied – not only in our work, but increasingly in the rest of our lives as well.

Our Beloved Hope: To Work Is to Love God by Loving Your Neighbors

Why did God design us to spend most of our time working? "This is really the open secret of all that follows," writes DeKoster at the start of the book. "Work is the form in which we make ourselves useful to others. ... That is why work gives meaning to life." (1)

We can work with hope because *to do good work is to love your neighbor.* Our work, whether paid or unpaid, skilled or unskilled, glamorous or unnoticed, serves human needs. It is by working, and only by working, that we are able to provide people with what they require to survive and thrive.

DeKoster asks us to imagine what would happen if those factory workers in his speech classes stopped working:

> Food vanishes from the store shelves, gas pumps dry up, streets are no longer patrolled, and fires burn themselves out. Communication and transportation services end and utilities go dead. Those who survive at all are soon huddled around campfires, sleeping in tents, and clothed in rags. The difference between barbarism and culture is, quite simply, work. (2-3)

Just imagine what this new perspective must have been like for those factory workers DeKoster taught. Your work has dignity and meaning, even in the face of all brokenness, because the survival of civilization itself depends on you! This is what it means to love your neighbor.

The impact our work has on our communities is one of those "larger realities" that defines the meaning of our work. We don't see it with our eyes every day, and if we lose our awareness of it, we lose the ability to do our work as a full expression of love for neighbor. Hence we must constantly draw the eyes of our souls back, and back again, to the larger world that our physical eyes can't see. (Pastors, take note – this is a lot easier if someone else prompts us to do it!)

However, work by itself is not enough. *Love for neighbor* by itself is not enough. Christians know that God is at the center of all, and must be at the center of our own lives. So if DeKoster is right that work is central to the meaning of our lives, where is God in our work?

God is present in and through our work, no matter how broken it is. God has put "making ourselves useful to others" at the center of life's meaning for two reasons: "First, God himself chooses to be served through the work that serves others. ... Second, God has so made us that through working we actually sculpt the kind of selves we each are becoming, in time and for eternity." (9)

To illustrate this twofold presence of God in our work, DeKoster turns to two familiar parables from Matthew 25: the Parable of the Sheep and the Goats (v. 31-46) and the Parable of the Talents (v. 14-30). At first, we might be tempted to focus on how "our work shapes ourselves for God" in the Parable of the Sheep and the Goats, and how "God is served by our work" in the Parable of the Talents. However, DeKoster shows that each of these themes is actually present in both parables.

Our Decisive Hope: Serving God and Shaping Self in the Parable of the Sheep and the Goats

DeKoster writes that for many years, he interpreted the Parable of the Sheep and the Goats as a call to support special programs and do religious works. Now, however, his thinking has changed:

> Once it seemed to commend special acts of giving, such as charities that we ought to be doing in our spare time. ... But now it seems to me that Jesus is obviously speaking of more than a vocational behavior or pastime kindness. Why? Because he hinges our entire eternal destiny upon giving ourselves to the service of others – and that can hardly be a pastime event. In fact, giving ourselves to the services of others, as obviously required by

the Lord, is precisely what the central block of life that we give to working turns out to be! (11)

The first of DeKoster's two modes of God's presence in our work – that God is served by it – is explicitly emphasized in the parable:

'I was hungry and you gave me something to eat.'

The Lord is saying that where humans are hungry, there he too chooses to hunger. He waits in the hungry man or woman or child, longing to be served. Served how? By the work of those who knit the garment of civilization through the production and distribution of food! (13)

Underneath this heading, DeKoster provides a lengthy list of occupations whose daily work is dedicated to feeding the hungry:

- Farmers, ranchers, and other agricultural workers
- Bakers, chefs, and other culinary workers
- Truckers, packers, and other transportation workers
- Wholesalers, retailers, and other commercial workers
- Kitchen and restaurant staff, and other hospitality workers
- All those who produce the tools and support services these professions need

... and so forth. The list is impressively long. When the roll is fully called, millions of people will be able to hear their daily work praised in the words, "I was hungry and you fed me."

DeKoster then goes down the list from the parable – "I was thirsty ... I needed clothes ... I was sick ... I was a stranger ... I was in prison ..." – and provides for each one a long list of occupations whose daily work is dedicated to meeting that need. It is all of us, through our daily work, who carry out these tasks. We can all work with hope because we are all serving Christ when we serve our neighbors' needs!

But don't the lost, or the "goats" of the parable, do this kind of work as well? Why wouldn't an unbelieving farmer or kitchen worker hear the same benediction, "I was hungry and you gave me something to eat"? The question brings us to the second mode of God's presence in our work: through our work, we shape ourselves for him.

What matters most to God is not that you go through the motions of doing work, but how and why you do it. In fact, the very reason it matters so much to God *whether* you work is because he cares so much about how and why you work!

In the parable, the saved and the lost are represented not simply as people with different track records, but as two different types of people. In real life, the difference between a sheep and a goat is not so much that they do different things as that they *are* different things. Similarly, DeKoster argues, the point of the parable is that God's people are different in kind from others.

The Son of Man pronounces his judgment simply by revealing to people what they truly are:

> The sheep got to the throne as already sheep; the goats got to the throne as already goats… The parable is teaching us that we will "see" at last what day-to-day-living is all about. (12)

> In the end, both sheep and goats are simply guided to the place they have been seeking all their lives: sheep are led to the company of the Lord they served, perhaps unknowingly; goats are assigned the place where goats alone belong – among their kind, in the alienation from each other and from God that they practiced in life. (19)

DeKoster reads the parable as a reflection on sanctification. Those who spend their lives serving God in their daily work will become, more and more, the kind of people who belong in God's sheepfold. They will develop a certain kind of character, Christian virtues, and spiritual formation. Meanwhile, those who spend their lives serving themselves will become, more and more, the kind of people who can find no place in God's sheepfold. Their sinful nature is given greater and greater expression in their lives, and is thus imprinted deeper and deeper in their characters.[39]

Our Fruitful Hope: Serving God and Shaping Self in the Parable of the Talents

The Parable of the Talents is one of the classic texts for contemplating the meaning of our daily work. However, many expositions of the parable don't get far beyond saying that God calls on us to work and attributes eternal significance to how well we answer that call. DeKoster uses the theme of God's twofold presence in our work to uncover some deeper layers of the parable.

---

[39] Unfortunately, as he focuses on sanctification, DeKoster is not always careful to keep in view the doctrines of regeneration and justification by faith apart from the works of the law. God's "sheep" do become more and more sheep-like over the course of their lives by doing the work of sheep. But it was not that kind of work, or any kind of work of their own, that made them sheep in the first place. They were born as goats, and it took a miracle of God to make them sheep. Moreover, the track record of good works that earns their place in heaven is not theirs, but Christ's. DeKoster knew all this, and near the end of the book he inserts what he calls a "theological note" to clarify that he has no intention of downplaying the Protestant understanding of regeneration and justification. (60-61) Still, it would have been preferable if he had touched on these themes more often, to keep the relationship between justification and sanctification more clear.

DeKoster reminds us that the divine calling to work implies that God himself is served by our work, and draws our attention to the democratizing, equalizing effect of this fact:

> The Master's intent is obvious: service. That's why each of the recipients of his largesse is called a servant. ... Notice, too, that the eye of heaven sees work in its essence, and takes small account of differences among jobs that we think are very important. Five-talent people look very "successful" by all worldly standards, stirring their pride and our envy; one-talent people risk our contempt and their own despair. But in the Master's eye "ratio" levels us all. ... No ground for pride; no excuse for envy. (24-25)

The modern economy, which creates large differences in financial rewards for different kinds of work, cannot be sustained culturally without this sense of equal dignity among "five-talent" and "one-talent" workers. The pride of the five-talent worker and the envy of the one-talent worker create social conflict that eventually becomes unsustainable – unless a spiritual influence works to mitigate that pride and envy.

The shaping of the self for God is also present in the parable. DeKoster shows how it illuminates the strict work ethic of the New Testament: "If anyone is not willing to work, let him not eat" (2 Thessalonians 3:10). Sloth is a sin because work is divine activity:

> The faithful servant is expected to work, you noticed, at full capacity. That, then, is the ratio that God blesses – full use of whatever talents we are given. Five-talent people are required to turn in a five-talent performance; so also with the two-talent folk, and so on. His is the choice as to our talents; ours is the duty to use them to the fullest. (24)

Here, again, the biblical view of work is a democratizing and equalizing force. DeKoster emphasizes that there is no significant distinction between the sloth of the rich man living off his wealth; the sloth of the middle-class slacker who puts in the minimum effort needed to get by; and the sloth of the poor man who finds panhandling or welfare more comfortable than a job. "On all such loafers, and any others, God takes a grim stand," DeKoster writes. (26)

But this biblical work ethic is no mere Pharisaical, legalistic condemnation of sloth. In the opening passage of this chapter, DeKoster provides his clearest and most powerful statement on how work "shapes the self" for God on a daily basis:

> The chisel we use to sculpt our selves is choice. It's not a chisel of our own making; it's a tool we can't avoid using. To live is to choose – even when we decline to choose, that is itself a choice. ... Do we choose what to think, what to say, what to do in obedience to our Creator's will? Or, do we choose

in obedience to self, or to any of the many other beguiling disguises worn by the Devil? We are always in the service of some "master" – ultimately, in the service of God or his Adversary. Obedience to God's will sculpts sheep, while rebellion molds goats.

And because work looms so large in a lifetime, the choices we make on the job play a decisive role in what kind of selves we are becoming. How do we sculpt our selves on the job? We do it with the chisel of choice, day by day. How well do we choose to do the work at hand? How well do we choose to develop and to use the talents God has given us? What is the quantity and quality of the work we choose to turn out, every hour? How do we choose – as employer or as employee – to relate to others on the job? (22)

Work is a crucible of character – a place where we become more and more the kind of people we already are in our hearts. That's why slothfulness is such serious business: it's a refusal to shape our selves for God. DeKoster explains: "Work is a duty. Why? Because God loans talents for the purpose of reaping return. Or, to put it another way: God loans us talents to enable us to choose the kind of self we will sculpt through using them." (27)

Our Steadfast Hope: Bearing the Cross for God's Glory

Don't get the wrong impression. For all this talk about how God is present with us in and through our work, DeKoster has not forgotten to connect with the brokenness and frustration of his audience. One of the great strengths of "Work" is the vivid portrait it paints of the toil and sorrow of daily work, and the message of hope and perseverance it brings to that world.

DeKoster devotes an entire chapter of his book to recording what he heard from those factory workers in his speech classes. "I have had some tutors of my own on the dark side of the job ... What a collection I might also compile of stories of blasted hopes and maimed spirits as recounted in sometimes halting tones from the speech platform." (29-30) He is careful to note that all people's work is broken, not just that of factory line workers. On the other hand, in light of our special duties to the poor and the marginalized, the challenges of the line worker are a worthy focus of attention.

One striking theme that emerges from DeKoster's account of the factory workers' lamentations goes beyond merely the pain and frustration of the daily burdens they bear. These workers want to know whether anyone cares. More painful than the physical and emotional strain are the deeper questions of meaning and relationship. Does it matter that I bear this? And does anyone care that I do?

Deep in their hearts, hurting and broken people want spiritual comfort – hope – more than they want material comfort. And that's a good thing, because according to Christianity, they actually need spiritual comfort much more than material comfort. The good news is, while material comfort is always expensive and often unattainable, spiritual comfort is available to all. It is a free gift for those who turn themselves over to God.

But while hope is free, it is not easy. DeKoster's starting point for bringing hope to broken work is the cross: "Christianity long ago took full account of the wounds we may suffer at work. 'If anyone would come after me, he must deny himself and take up his cross daily and follow me'" (Luke 9:23). (35) Just as Jesus gave himself up to be broken, we must give ourselves up to be broken.

The answer to the broken worker's cry, "Does anybody care?" is a resounding "Yes!" Yes, God cares. He cares immeasurably for the worker who continues to show up faithfully to the toilsome, frustrating job that serves his community and keeps civilization running. When we take up our cross daily and bear it in our work, we please God.

This "yes" contains one of the most important fulfillments of God's promises of hope. Christian hope is not only for the eschaton; while the final consummation of hope is in the future, the firstfruits of hope are already present with us. To please God gives us dignity and meaning, even in the midst of the most broken situations.

DeKoster connects cross-bearing – perseverance under trial – to his earlier themes of work serving others and shaping the self. In one of the most moving passages in the book, DeKoster asks us to consider how the persevering workers of his world must look from God's perspective:

> As the Lord surveys his world, what a host of rugged heroes and heroines of labor he must behold! Those who rise with the sun, lifelong, to jobs that demand endless self-sacrifice, and get in return but little reward in pay and still less in recognition. Those who see no sunshine all the day long, in the caverns of the earth or the noisome dungeons of heavy industry. And those – no less heroic – who find their substantial salary and bonuses but small recompense for the burdens, and the envy, their "success" involves. Those who must day by day drive weary bodies and spent minds to one more effort. Those who wrestle with bureaucracy to keep businesses solvent long after patience and pleasure are dead. Some who exercise initiative without appreciation, but persevere well beyond the need for personal monetary reward. Mothers whose lives are poured into their families; fathers whose bodies are sacrificed that their wives and children might live. God sees migrant families struggling hopelessly from dawn to dusk; peasants who grub like slaves without hope; service employees called any time for emergencies, surrendering their family holidays or busy through the dark of night.

"Lose your life," is Jesus asking us? [Luke 9:24] He is talking about the martyrdoms of labor, too. (37)

It is the shaping of ourselves in this perseverance that earns the Lord's "well done" in the Parable of the Talents, the benediction that provides our lives with the only eternal meaning and purpose they can ultimately have. And it is the weaving of civilization from the threads of our work, as we serve one another's needs, that grounds the Lord's "you did it unto me" in the Parable of the Sheep and the Goats. The fallen world is a world of hunger, sickness, and strangers; our work feeds, heals, and welcomes our fellow human beings in need. Hope is not just for individuals seeking dignity and meaning; it is for communities seeking to flourish.

Our Unchanging Hope: The Two-Edged Swords of Technology and Globalization

The continuing advance of technology is one of the most important factors shaping work in the modern world. It enables us to serve human needs far more effectively, lifting millions around the world out of poverty, hunger, disease, and death. At the same time, technology's power to reshape our work can have bad effects as well as good ones. Ever since the emergence of the modern factory in the 18th century, some observers have worried that the conditions of work in modernity must inevitably be unnatural and inhumane. Technology has also brought about the globalization of markets, extending economic relationships to the point where almost everyone in the world can do business with one another. This, too, has produced many benefits and many anxieties.

DeKoster took a keen interest in these subjects, partly because they were so critical to the challenges facing the factory workers in his classes. His approach is a strange mix of optimism and pessimism. On both sides of that ledger, he has important things to say. Yet his optimism is sometimes too optimistic, and his pessimism is sometimes too pessimistic.

When he contemplates the good that is – and can be – accomplished by technology and globalization, he is effusive:

It's simply far better to be one of the workers tending the needs of a huge mechanical harvester as part of some vast agribusiness than to live in a world where starvation stalks its millions of victims. Technology makes it possible to produce enough food now around the world to feed everyone … Technology has revolutionized civilization, and it promises untold achievements ahead! The work that serves it weaves the fabric of culture. (43-44)

The benefits are more than just material; they are spiritual. We are now in meaningful relationships with millions of people around the world through economic exchange. The material benefit is that those people do not starve; the spiritual benefit is that we now work together with them as fellow human beings. "Work ranges far ahead of politics in bringing the peoples of the globe closer together. The multinational corporations ... draw diverse sinews of labor into cooperative and constructive effort which transcends geographic boundaries, penetrates political borders, and even joins East and West, North and South." (39)

Paradoxically, at the same time that he is offering these optimistic encouragements, DeKoster seems to agree with the critics who think technology makes the conditions of work less humane. He argues that this is the price we must pay for the blessings technology lets us create for our fellow human beings. He offers no assurance that as progress continues this price will not end up being quite high. "Those who pay for technological achievements by serving the robots give just that much more of themselves to cross-bearing for human progress." (44) He bluntly tells us, in effect, to suck it up and pay the price, for our neighbors' sake as well as our own.

There is much value in DeKoster's perspective on technological change. On the optimistic side, new technologies and global markets do give us a breathtaking, unprecedented power to love our neighbors and contribute to worldwide human flourishing. From 1970 to 2006, the portion of the world's population living on a dollar per day or less dropped 80 percent. Literally a billion people rose out of that level of extreme poverty. Living standards have doubled globally.[40] More importantly, this progress has been achieved in part through an unprecedented expansion of respect for human rights and the building of relationships between cultures.[41]

The overall biblical narrative gives us good grounds for hope that technological advancement is not intrinsically evil or disordering. Nature was given to humanity in the beginning so that our work could transform it for the better. That is what we are seeing today as billions around the world emerge from poverty, thanks to technology and globalization.

DeKoster's realism about technological change also gives us food for thought. It is healthy to be reminded that we can't have it all. DeKoster is right when he says that even if technological advancement has some downsides, the alternative is mass starvation and barbarism. Are we prepared to condemn millions of people in Africa, India, and China to die so we can have the luxury of pursuing our romantic visions of traditional agricultural life?

---

[40] Maxim Pinkovskiy and Xavier Sala-i-Martin, "Parametric Estimations of the World Distribution of Income," National Bureau of Economic Research, October 2009, http://www.nber.org/papers/w15433.

[41] See Wayne Grudem and Barry Asmus, "The Poverty of Nations" (Wheaton: Crossway, 2013).

And yet, DeKoster's optimism sometimes carries him too far. At one point in the book, he even seems to offer overconfident promises of global peace and prosperity. (39-40) We need not go that far! Hope is a Christian virtue, but naiveté about the brokenness of the world is not. While the potential of technology and globalization is very great, it is a two-edged potential. God never owes us success.[42]

We also need not fully accept DeKoster's flat, suck-it-up pessimism about dehumanized work environments. Here, for once, he is insufficiently hopeful. A robust Christian hope, no matter how tempered by realism, does not leave room for simply accepting the dominion of brokenness. Even common sense will tell us that an economic order built exclusively on cross-bearing will be unsustainable in the long run.

However, more than just a deficiency of hope is at work. DeKoster's views are shaped by the books of economic and sociological scholars – Adam Smith, Karl Marx, Max Weber, and their scholarly successors – who did not accurately keep track of the real empirical effects of technological change. While the initial disruptions of traditional agricultural life in the 18th century created many inhumane work practices, over time technology has tended to make the conditions of work more humane, rather than less so.

In a fallen world that is under the curse of Genesis 3:17-19, the most "natural" condition of work is back-breaking, highly repetitive field labor, starting in early childhood and continuing without interruption until death. Industrialization has not, overall, made working conditions worse. In the long run, it has made them much better – and much more humane.

So while some people in some situations may be called to the kind of extraordinary sacrifice DeKoster describes, this does not need to be the normal situation. The working population in general should not give up its humanity, even to feed the world – and at this point, all indications are that no such sacrifice will, in fact, be demanded. In the 18th century, pastoral leaders such as John Wesley embraced the Industrial Revolution and affirmed the legitimacy of the modern, entrepreneurial economy that was emerging. But they also fought to reform practices such as child labor or workplaces that were unsafe or unsanitary. We can do the same, embracing technology and globalization for their benefits, without turning our consciences over to them.

---

[42] It is possible DeKoster's overly optimistic expectations for global peace and prosperity are influenced by postmillennial eschatology. If so, those who don't take the postmillennial view would do well to make charitable allowances for theological differences before judging him too harshly. But they can still, with charity, decline to join him in his more effusive predictions.

Our Shared Hope: Community, Freedom, and Responsibility in the Social Order

"The end of it all," DeKoster writes, is "executive stewardship." God has made human beings – both as individuals and collectively in communities – to manage and cultivate the creation order. By the word "executive," he stresses the role of human mind, will, and conscience. "That's what an executive is: one who makes decisions." We are thinking and choosing creatures, morally responsible for our actions. This mysterious agency and responsibility is central to who we are as image-bearers. By the word "stewardship," he stresses that our agency is made to be used in service to God, for his glory. We do make decisions as the world's resident executives, but "the good executive only executes the will of others." (57)

Executive stewardship raises the final, big question DeKoster takes on in "Work" – the nature of community. In the final sections of the book, he turns from the task of encouraging individual workers to see their work as part of a larger social whole, and takes up the nature of the whole itself. We are all, individually, executive stewards. But we are also members of a community, and to do our work well, we must begin with that in mind. So what does a community of executive stewards look like?

This question would seem to present us with an unsolvable problem. If each individual is an executive, pursuing his or her own personal vision of stewardship, how can all of our work fit together and weave a civilization? But if we take away that personal agency and authority from the worker, haven't we stripped the individual of his or her status as an executive steward? How do we respect the image of God in each individual while holding the community together?

These questions are no less pressing today than they were in 1982. Granted, the context has changed. DeKoster encountered these questions in part through the Cold War confrontation between capitalism and communism. This background should be borne in mind when reading DeKoster, because it shaped some of his analysis – as was the case in virtually all writing on the topic of work during the Cold War era.

But DeKoster also encountered these questions through the sense of powerlessness and loss of identity he met in those factory workers. *That* context has not changed much. It demanded an answer then and still demands one today. Even the larger social and historical questions that shaped the Cold War – Can a nation be free and have community at the same time? – remain relevant for our communities today.

Work ought to have a context of freedom. Only if work is done freely can it fully express love for neighbor and shape us into the kind of people God wants us to be. Freedom does not mean anarchism or libertarianism. It means treating people as executive stewards – as stewards over all that rightfully lies within their sphere of control and influence – which is exactly what God says they are.

At the most immediate level, the executive stewardship of the individual and the needs of the community meet through economic exchange. Each of us does his or her job, providing for the needs of others. Each of us gets paid for this work, and we use the wages to acquire the goods and services created by other people's work.

This exchange also requires a context of freedom if it is to be done in love. As DeKoster profoundly puts it, "Work and wage draw together at the point where conscience functions." (57) Work is inextricably linked with economic exchange, and conscience sits atop the connection governing both. But only if we are given freedom to live as executive stewards can our daily work and wage fully provide the opportunity for conscience to function effectively.

How, then, can free people have community? The starting point is that *work and exchange create community by creating harmony and peace.* Work heals broken relationships and forges a shared sense of identity and purpose. "Our work joins us in knitting the garment of culture which we ourselves enjoy." (39) When people work together, and even when they engage in economic exchange, they join in a common cause toward a shared goal. This implicitly recognizes the humanity of others. We recognize that we need each other.

Both sides of the ledger – work and wage – draw the executive stewardship of each individual into the service of the community. I take my job freely (rather than being forced to do a job that was chosen for me, as under socialist systems) and do the work as an expression of my own agency. I buy and sell as a steward of my money and goods, in a marketplace that is not under the arbitrary control of a central planner. Yet in both the work and the wage, the needs of my neighbors are served.

DeKoster asks us to consider how thousands of people, who don't even know each other, work together to create all the objects we use every day:

> That chair you are lounging in? Could you have made it for yourself? Well, I suppose so, if we mean just the chair! Perhaps you did in fact go out to buy the wood, the nails, the glue, the stuffing, the springs – and put it all together. But if by making a chair we mean assembling each part from scratch, that's quite another matter. How do we get, say, the wood? Go and fell a tree? But only after first making the tools for that, and putting together some kind of vehicle to haul the wood, and constructing a mill to do the lumber, and roads to drive on from place to place?

> In short, a lifetime or two to make one chair! We are physically unable, it is obvious, to provide ourselves from scratch with the household goods

we can now see from wherever you and I are sitting – to say nothing of building and furnishing the whole house.

Consider everything else that we can use every day and never really see. Who builds and maintains the roads and streets we take for granted? Who polices them so we can move about in comparative safety? Who erects the stores, landscapes the parks, builds the freeways? Who provides the services that keep things going in good weather and bad?

Well, civilization blends work together into all that. ... There are countless workers, just like ourselves – including ourselves – whose work creates the harvest that provides each of us with far more than we could ever provide for ourselves. (4)

But here we must be very careful. Markets are not some machine that delivers good outcomes automatically. DeKoster was no pedantic peddler of economic ideology, treating systems as if they had no relationship to the people operating within them.

The whole package – shared work creating peace and harmony, markets reconciling freedom and community – works *only* if people possess moral character and the economic system is just. A nation of cheats and scoundrels is not going to grow more harmonious through shared work. And even the peace created by good people working together will be undermined if the system within which they work rewards cheats and scoundrels. We don't have to be perfect people or have a perfect system, but we do have to be good enough people with a good enough system.

Freedom, responsibility, and community are interdependent. The freedom to take what you want rather than serve the common good is not true freedom at all. As DeKoster pointedly asks: "When are we 'free' to use the highways? When we [all] drive as we please? No, *only* when most drivers maintain order by obeying most of the laws most of the time. Destroy the system so we drive as we please, and, of course, no one would really be free to use the road." (45)

True freedom is *voluntary lawfulness*. When people freely choose to work for one another's benefit, they are free to live in community. It is their responsibility to each other that sets them free.

With this perspective on freedom, we can recover our agency and responsibility even in situations where they seem the most lost. If freedom means the power to do whatever you want, factory workers have little of it. But if freedom is a voluntary lawfulness that chooses to serve the needs of others, they can find freedom in their work, and in the economic exchange their work empowers them for.

DeKoster's Three Dimensions of Work

While it seems simple and plainspoken on the surface, DeKoster's book actually invites us to view work as a complex, three-dimensional reality. These dimensions are neither simple nor straightforward in practice; real life always defies the simplicity of our schemes of classification. However, this three-dimensional rubric can help us intentionally broaden our thinking and become aware of aspects of work that we may not have otherwise considered.

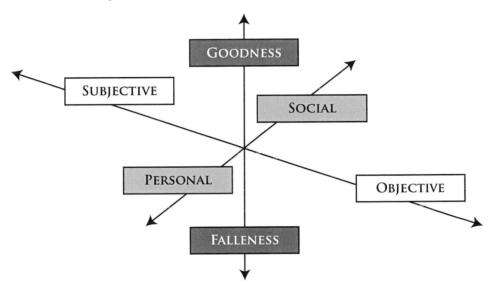

One dimension of our work is defined by the distinction between the *objective* and *subjective*. No matter how pious our feelings about it are, it still matters to God whether our work is actually having a beneficial effect on other people. At the same time, human dignity and the shaping of the self for God can only be lived out if we do our work with the right sense of identity and motives. We see this dimension most clearly in DeKoster's twofold understanding of God's presence in our work: We love God in our work by serving our neighbor (objectively) and shaping ourselves (subjectively).

The second dimension is defined by *goodness* and *fallenness*. Theologically, the goodness of God in our work must be primary, lest we compromise our conception of his transcendence or deny the gospel truth that Christ has overcome the world. But for many people, the daily experience of work is overwhelmed by the brokenness of the Fall and the curse. The Christian virtue of hope addresses itself to the experience of suffering and evil with a message of victory and light.

The third dimension is defined by the *personal* and *social*. Each individual is an executive steward with agency and responsibility. We must not turn inward and use our work or our wages as opportunities to serve ourselves, but must use them to serve the needs of our households and communities. The community, in turn, must honor each individual as an executive steward, sustaining systems of work and exchange that are just and provide the necessary context of freedom and responsibility.

The faith and work movement is reaching a new level of maturity. It first emerged among workers who felt called to affirm the goodness of God in their work. Now it is beginning to reach a wider world of workers, many of whom feel little connection to these cheerful affirmations. The hopeful, three-dimensional vision of Lester DeKoster can help pastors discover new directions for growth, shining the light of Christ into a dark and dying world.

REFLECTION QUESTIONS

1. DeKoster writes that he once thought the Parable of the Sheep and the Goats primarily referred to "special acts of giving, such as charities that we ought to be doing in our spare time." Why did he come to view this interpretation as inadequate?

2. How can the Parable of the Talents help us understand the Bible's strict work ethic as something beautiful that gives dignity and meaning to life, rather than a mere Pharisaical demand?

3. When speaking to people whose work is characterized by suffering or discouragement, what are some good starting points for connecting our message to their experience? What are appropriate goals for the pastoral care of such workers?

4. Why does the ordinary worker need to be regularly reminded of how his work affects his community? Why do communities need to be regularly reminded of what their workers contribute?

Made for
WORSHIP

Jay Slocum

We're made for worship as well as work, and the two don't have to be at odds. Work is a form of worship; in fact, the same Hebrew word (*avodah*) is used in the Old Testament to mean both "work" and "worship." The special kind of worship that happens on Sunday morning, apart from the world of work, is unique and indispensable. However, the local church cannot obey the Great Commission to "make disciples" if it does not also equip people to do their work as worship all week long. In this trenchant essay, Jay Slocum lays out many practical lessons he has learned over the years as he has labored to bring this integration of work and worship into the life of the local church.

Jay Slocum is the rector of Jonah's Call Anglican Church in Pittsburgh, Pa. The church draws its name from God's instructions to Jonah that he must go to the city of the lost to bear witness. Jonah's Call is Slocum's third church plant. Slocum earned his M.Div. from Trinity Episcopal School for Ministry. He is also highly active in the faith and work movement in Pittsburgh. Before becoming a pastor, he worked for 10 years providing services to the disabled. He describes himself as "an audio and bibliophile, an avid BMXer and mountain bike rider, a foodie, a design geek, and a cultural omnivore."

How Do We Change Our Habits?

Everyone knows that worship is central to the local church. But for most people, "worship" usually means gathering to worship on Sunday morning and nothing more. Obviously, gathering for worship within the church is essential. But people are made to worship God in everything they do. The gathered worship that takes place inside the church building must not only be a time of worship for its own sake; it must also prepare Christians to worship in everything they do throughout the week.

Unfortunately, a lot of churches have developed bad worship habits. Many Christians – including seminary professors, pastors, and committed lay leaders – are seeking reform. Getting churches to change is a daunting task. But we serve a great God who has given us both the local and universal church for a good reason. Relying on his grace, reform is possible, and the results are well worth it.

Many westerners within the church habitually separate their facts from their values, as well as their private and public lives. This fact-value split occurs when we take the stance that hard, quantifiable facts belong in the public sphere, while "soft" qualities like religious values or supernatural beliefs belong in the private sphere. This fact-value split divides Sunday from the rest of the week, the church from the rest of life. Sunday is sacred, but Monday through Saturday is secular.

We support this sacred-secular divide when we encourage lay people to "pay, pray, and stay out of the way." The professionalization of roles within the church can lead us to classify missionaries, pastors, church staffers, and lay workers on a decreasing scale of godliness. Missionaries get gold medals, pastors get silver, and church staffers get bronze. Christian lawyers and engineers get rude jokes about how they're cheats and they're boring – often straight from the pulpit.

Moreover, within the sacred-secular divide, we build churches of all sizes that are busy, fun, and safe from the world, but somehow do not seem capable of changing our communities, or helping us live our lives in vibrant ways anywhere except in the church. We have meetings, events, and activities that fill up our week, making it ever so hard to make sense of, integrate, or engage our families, neighborhoods, occupations, coworkers, or cities.

These habits have left the church reeling in a world where Christendom no longer dominates the landscape. So, how do we change them?

How to Change? Therapy and the 12 Steps

Changing the habits of the church requires a two-pronged approach. First, we must uncover the lies we believe and reject them for truths that will set us free. As Jesus says, "If you hold to my teaching, you are really my disciples. Then you will know the truth, and the truth will set you free" (John 8:31-32). Second, we must decide to live another way. Jesus says as well: "Whoever practices and teaches these commands will be called great in the kingdom of heaven. For I tell you that unless your righteousness surpasses that of the Pharisees and the teachers of the law, you will certainly not enter the kingdom of heaven" (Matthew 5:19b-20).

There seem be two schools of thought at work in the world of behavioral change. Some agents of change focus on our thoughts and core beliefs as the key. I once heard a counselor say: "There is no point in using paper towels to clean up a spill in your kitchen if it is coming from an overflowing sink. Instead, go to the faucet, turn off the running water, unclog the sink, and then get some paper towels to finish the job." It is a fitting metaphor for what many therapists and counselors do with their patients – get to the core belief that is keeping a person from changing so that new behavior will follow.

At the opposite end of the spectrum is the school that believes that change occurs through action and ritual, leading to belief. Twelve-step communities from Alcoholics Anonymous to Overeaters Anonymous fully embody this approach. Attend any 12-step meeting and you are likely to hear phrases like "little by slowly," "fake it 'til you make it," and "you can't think your way into a new way of living; you have to live your way into a new way of thinking."

In the grand scheme of things, it appears that both of these methods achieve results. Why not try both at the same time? In the past 20 years, it has been my experience that changing core beliefs to produce new behavior (psychotherapy or inner healing prayer), as well as changing behavior to produce new thinking (12-step programs and church liturgies) are both highly effective ways to create change in people's lives.

Thinking Worldview-ishly and Making Culture

These two approaches to behavioral change are also present in the church. From the presuppositional apologetics of Cornelius Van Til[43] to the cultural analysis of Francis Schaeffer,[44] one school seeks to change our way of thinking so that we might change our way of living. In his book "Escape from Reason," Schaeffer points out that "Christianity provides a unified answer for the whole of life." He then shows the world, the church, and the academy many ways to analyze a thought system or worldview so that cultural change can occur. This approach to change (belief to behavior) has filtered down into the work of thinkers and

---

[43] Cornelius Van Til's book, "Christian Apologetics" (Phillipsburg: P&R Publishing Co., 2003.), is easier to read about than to actually read. However, it is a hallmark for those who approach apologetics from a presuppositional perspective.

[44] In his books, "Escape from Reason" (Downers Grove: InterVarsity Press, 2006) and "How Shall We Then Live" (Wheaton: Crossway Books, 2005). Francis Schaeffer popularized presuppositional apologetics and made Van Til's approach to addressing false beliefs accessible to many pastors, teachers, and lay people.

cultural change agents like Chuck Colson,[45] Os Guinness,[46] and myriad others who occupy positions within the intellectual community and the church.

At the popular level, Rick Warren uses this type of approach to advocate how we change our behavior. Warren says:

> You've got to start with the belief – the lie – behind the behavior ... The way you think determines the way you feel, and the way you feel determines the way you act. If you want to change the way you act, you must determine the way you think. You can't start with the action. You've got to start with the thought.[47]

At the opposite end of the spectrum is the emerging school that tells us the way to change is through action, or more broadly, through making culture. Andy Crouch, in his recent book "Culture Making: Recovering Our Creative Calling," challenges the "worldview" approach:

> The language of worldview tends to imply, to paraphrase the Catholic writer Richard Rohr, that we can think ourselves into new ways of behaving. But that is not the way culture works. Culture helps us behave ourselves into new ways of thinking. The risk in thinking "worldviewishly" is that we will start to think that the best way to change culture is to analyze it. We will start worldview academies, host worldview seminars, write worldview books. These may have some real value if they help us understand the horizons that our culture shapes, but they cannot substitute for the creation of real cultural goods. And they will subtly tend to produce philosophers rather than plumbers, abstract thinkers instead of artists and artisans. They can create a cultural niche in which "worldview thinkers" are privileged while other kinds of culture makers are shunted aside. But culture is not changed simply by thinking.[48]

Whether it is a layperson seeking to change his or her behavior, or a seminary professor or pastor seeking to create social or cultural change, might we be highly effective in changing our habits by tackling both our thoughts and actions at the same time?

Belief-Changing Behavior, Behavior-Changing Belief

If we wish to be a people set free from the habits that separate the private from the public and the church from the world, we must see what God says in his

---

[45] Colson wrote "How Now Shall We Live?" (Wheaton: Tyndale House Publishers, 1999) with Nancy Pearcey.

[46] See Os Guinness, "The Call: Finding and Fulfilling the Central Purpose of Your Life" (Nashville: W Publishing Group, 2003), which is written from a "worldview-ish" perspective.

[47] Rick Warren, "9 Preaching Tips that Will Save Lives," Church Leaders, 2014, http://www.churchleaders.com/pastors/pastor-articles/151787-warren-9-preaching-tips-that-will-save-lives.html.

[48] Andy Crouch, "Culture Making: Recovering Our Creative Calling" (Downers Grove: InterVarsity Press, 2008), 256.

Word about how we ought to think about the church, the world, and the cultures in which we live. Though there are certainly far more, I offer 10 areas where big ideas can lead to big changes in the ordering of our lives within the church, and consequently, areas where the church can help bring order to the world.

This list of big areas is not a new "10-step program" for pastors to implement. Every church needs to discern its own needs. God takes care of his churches, and every church needs to rely on God, not somebody's program. But in two decades of working on this problem within the church, this is what I've learned so far.

My 10 big areas are:

1. Being Salt and Light
2. Upholding the Cultural Mandate
3. Practicing Common Grace for the Common Good
4. Defining Work Biblically
5. Living Out of God's Four-fold Pattern for the Gospel
6. Instilling Worship in All Things
7. Being Stewards of All Aspects of Life
8. Responding to God's Calling in All of Our Work
9. Participating in God's Mission to Save the World
10. Being Church With a Vocationally Infused Vision and Mission

1. Being Salt and Light

In Matthew 5:13-16, Jesus said to the church:

> You are the salt of the earth. But if the salt loses its saltiness, how can it be made salty again? It is no longer good for anything, except to be thrown out and trampled by men. You are the light of the world. A city on a hill cannot be hidden. Neither do people light a lamp and put it under a bowl. Instead they put it on its stand, and it gives light to everyone in the house. In the same way, let your light shine before men, that they may see your good deeds and praise your Father in heaven.

In this passage, Jesus employs both a negative and positive metaphor. In the negative metaphor, he speaks of us being salt, which preserves things from rotting. In the other, he uses the metaphor of light, which reveals something hidden and allows us to see clearly. In his commentary on this passage, the great Anglican theologian John Stott says:

> Jesus calls his disciples to exert a double influence on the society – a negative influence by arresting its decay and a positive influence by bringing light

into its darkness. For it is one thing to stop the spread of evil; it is another to promote the spread of truth, beauty and goodness.[49]

Some of us who come from a fundamentalist or Anabaptist tradition have seen the power of a church that is clearly defined as church. In these traditions, we are good at being salt by maintaining a clear sense of holiness, piety, and the divine. Some of us who come from a reformed evangelical tradition have witnessed the power of the church as one that reaches into the world by creating or reforming institutions. Presbyterian preacher and teacher Tim Keller commented on this tendency to be salt *or* light, offering us a corrective in a 2006 interview:

> I think when Jesus says salt and light, that means there is darkness in the world and we are being the light, and the salt images means that there is decay in the culture and we are being a preservative and we're keeping the culture from decay. Even if you are a Stanley Haurwas-type[50] who believes that you're not supposed to be trying to put Christian ethics into public policy at all ... He would still say that by Christians starting churches, developing churches and doing evangelism and creating these great Christian counter-cultures that are committed to holiness, chastity, generosity, and compassion for the poor, that we are redeeming the culture. They are being salt that keeps it from decay and light because they are lifting up the right way to be human rather than the wrong way to be human. And if you are a Kuyperian[51] type who believes that we are supposed to take our Christian worldview and work our way into every area of culture from art to government as Christians, we are redeeming culture. ... It seems to me that ... the cultural transformationists (from Kuyper to Calvin College) have underemphasized the importance of thick, strong Christian communities that serve as Christian counter-cultures. The Anabaptists and the Haurwasians, they put all the emphasis on really strong counter cultures that show the world how people ought to live rather than bringing your Christian Worldview into the culture. I can't see how we can't do both.

---

[49] John R. W. Stott, "The Message of the Sermon on the Mount" (Downers Grove: Inter-Varsity Press, 1978), 64-65.

[50] Stanley Haurwas and William H. Willimon, "Resident Aliens: Life in the Christian Colony" (Nashville: Abingdon Press, 1989). The authors say: "Christians must again understand that their first task is not to make the world better or more just ... The first social task of the church is to provide the space and time necessary for developing skills [that] help us recognize the possibilities and limitations of our society. In developing such skills, the church and Christians must be uninvolved in the politics of our society and involved in the polity that is the church. For the Christian, therefore, the church is always the primary polity through which we gain the experience to negotiate and make positive contributions to whatever society in which we may find ourselves."

[51] Abraham Kuyper is famously and relentlessly quoted as saying, "There is not a square inch in the whole domain of our human existence over which Christ, who is sovereign over all, does not cry: mine!"

Each tradition tends to be weak because it doesn't do the other [act as salt and light].[52]

So are we with theologian Haurwas and third century Church Father Tertullian, who demands that we be salt by shouting, "What has Athens to do with Jerusalem or the Academy with the Church? Nothing!"[53] Or do we stand beside Dutch Prime Minister Abraham Kuyper and English Parliamentarian William Wilberforce, who, desiring to be light, proclaimed, "God Almighty has set before me two great objects, the suppression of the slave trade and the reformation of manners"?[54]

When my wife Catherine and I planted Jonah's Call in 2008 with a committed group of lay leaders, we discovered firsthand that it isn't just one or the other. At first, we had a thoroughly Kuyperian vision for our church. The masthead of our blog read, "All Things Renewed." However, two years into our plant, we realized we had focused so much on being light that our proverbial roast was rotting in the fridge. When core leaders begin to think the institutional church that gathers on Sunday morning is of little value compared to the worship they offer in their primary vocations within the city, you have a problem. When folks give so much time, money, and effort to loving the city that the church begins to look like a starving child, it's time to regroup. Believe it or not, a church with a vigorous missional mindset, intent on making the city a great place to live and the culture a place where God's kingdom comes, can overstate its case. We did. As a result, we needed more salt to keep folks grounded in the distinctive community of the church gathered, rather than just the church scattered.

Our course correction included rethinking how we described the church; we stopped using the phrase "faith community" and began to refer to ourselves as Jonah's Call Anglican Church. In keeping with Anglican tradition, I now wear a clergy collar as a regular aspect of my vocational calling to the priesthood within the church. We have added, along with a regular sermon series on work and culture, sermon series that address our role within the body, and the importance of institutions to shape us while we shape institutions.

Churches with different ecclesiologies will approach this problem differently. What's important is that our churches find ways to be holy, preserving communities, as well as sending, serving communities. As we form and reform churches that suffer from a sacred-secular divide, we will do well to simply follow the teaching of Jesus, working to preserve and transform at the same time.

---

[52] Tim Keller interviewed at the Desiring God Conference, 2006, http://www.youtube.com/watch?v=i1Q6Zun2v-8.

[53] Tertullian's (AD 160-220) famous statement in chapter seven of De praescriptione haereticorum (On the Prescription of Heretics).

[54] William Wilberforce (1759-1833) is chiefly credited for his role in the abolition of slavery in England in the 19th century. When he says the reformation of manners, he means broad social reform across England.

What's Happening in Your Church?

- Does your church use the language of "going into full-time ministry" to describe church-paid workers (pastors, missionaries, etc.), or do you see all vocations offered as acts of worship as full-time ministry?

- Does your church tell stories in which the only heroes are church-paid workers?

2. Upholding the Cultural Mandate

In Genesis 1:28, God says, "Be fruitful and increase in number; fill the earth and subdue it. Rule over the fish of the sea and the birds of the air and over every living creature that moves on the ground." Commenting on this passage, Nancy Pearcey identifies what is commonly known as the cultural mandate:

> In Genesis, God gives what we might call the first job description: "Be fruitful and multiply and fill the earth and subdue it." The first phrase, "be fruitful and multiply" means to develop the social world: build families, churches, schools, cities, governments, laws. The second phrase, "subdue the earth," means to harness the natural world: plant crops, build bridges, design computers, compose music. This passage is sometimes called the Cultural Mandate because it tells us that our original purpose was to create cultures, build civilizations – nothing less.[55]

Because making culture was core to Adam's identity as the first human, it follows that it is core to who we are as humans. Hence, it will do us well in the church to include the cultural mandate as a key tenant in the discipling of converts and witnessing to the rest of humanity. We must save souls, but a key component of salvation is the restoration of humanity to a right understanding of what we were made for – to cooperate with God by bringing flourishing into the world (rather than diminishing it) as an ongoing act of worship.

It will not do us any good, however, to merely share how important it is for us to make culture. We must also teach our people that cultures make us. This already happens inside the church: we adopt certain practices, such as encouraging people to bring Bibles to worship because these practices help shape the kind of people we become. We should also help people become aware of how culture outside the church shapes us.

An example of this in action is the Apprenticeship Series at Jonah's Call. In this program, we walk with teens through various businesses and institutions, showing them the ways these entities express their vision for life through the products they offer, the ways they operate, and the rituals and habits they uphold

---

[55] Nancy Pearcey, "Total Truth: Liberating Christianity from Its Cultural Captivity" (Wheaton: Crossway Books, 2004), 47.

to shape customers and patrons. From the library to the coffee shop, we help teens see that it is God's desire for us to make things that add to human flourishing. The things we eat, wear, and experience shape us in ways that either help us flourish or diminish our lives.

What's Happening in Your Church?
- Does your church intentionally institute or remove rituals or habits so that it can help form people into the kinds of Christians it is seeking to produce?
- Can the average parishioner in your church explain what it means to shape culture and how we are shaped by it?

3. Practice Common Grace for the Common Good

Psalm 145:9 states, "The Lord is good to all, and his mercies are over all his works." In his Sermon on the Mount, Jesus commands us to love our enemies saying: "But I tell you, love your enemies and pray for those who persecute you, that you may be children of your Father in heaven. He causes his sun to rise on the evil and the good, and sends rain on the righteous and the unrighteous" (Matthew 5:44-45). The doctrine of common grace is embedded in these passages. This doctrine was solidified by the Christian Reformed Church's 1924 synodical decision, which states:

> There is indeed a kind of non-salvific attitude of divine favor toward all human beings, manifested in three ways: (1) the bestowal of natural gifts, such as rain and sunshine, upon creatures in general, (2) the restraining of sin in human affairs, so that the unredeemed do not produce all of the evil that their depraved natures might otherwise bring about, and (3) the ability of unbelievers to perform acts of civic good.[56]

Common grace is God's work to maintain his created order and to restrain the powers of sin and Satan from destroying both his creatures and creation. This is an important doctrine in our present setting because common grace allows us to partner with people who have not experienced saving grace, and who are natural enemies of God and his people.

In Jeremiah 29:4-7, we hear the prophet command a people in exile. He says:

> This is what the Lord Almighty, the God of Israel, says to all those I carried into exile from Jerusalem to Babylon: "Build houses and settle down; plant gardens and eat what they produce. Marry and have sons and daughters; find wives for your sons and give your daughters in marriage, so that they too may have sons and daughters. Increase in number there; do not

---

[56] David K. Naugle, "Christianity and Popular Culture," BreakPoint, Spring 2003, http://www.breakpoint.org/features-columns/articles/breakpoint-features-search/entry/12/9503.

decrease. Also, seek the peace and prosperity of the city to which I have carried you into exile. Pray to the Lord for it, because if it prospers, you too will prosper.

From Joseph to Daniel, one of the key ways that God reached the lost was through the faithfulness of his people. Particularly when his people are in exile, God desires us to seek the welfare of the city, rather than create ghettos where we hide from the culture, or on the other extreme, totally assimilate the values and habits of the culture. Today, many of us argue that we have much in common with the exilic people of God. And, as a result, we look to Scripture for guidance as we seek to serve God as strangers in a strange land. One of the ways we can love God and love our neighbor is to serve the common good just as Jeremiah instructed God's people centuries ago.

When we combine common grace with common good, we create a powerful means of engaging the world and making culture that brings flourishing to the world. This stance allows us to act as both salt and light to our unsaved families, neighbors, cities, and world.

It is this combined strategy to reach the lost that causes Keller to observe:

> It will not be enough for Christians to form a culture that runs counter to the values of the broader culture. Christians should be a community radically committed to the good of the city as a whole. We must move out to sacrificially serve the good of the whole human community, especially the poor. Revelation 21-22 makes it clear that the ultimate purpose of redemption is not to escape the material world but to renew it. God's purpose is not only to save individuals but also to inaugurate a new world based on justice, peace, and love, not power, strife, and selfishness.[57]

I recently visited an eye doctor who asked me what I do for a living. I said, "I am a pastor of a church."

He responded: "Oh, I am an atheist. Where do you pastor?"

I told him that I pastor a church in Pittsburgh called Jonah's Call Anglican Church.

He replied: "I grew up Jewish in Squirrel Hill, so I know Jonah. Why Jonah's Call?"

"Well," I said, "the name comes from Jonah 4:11 where God says to Jonah, 'How can I not be concerned about that great city full of people who do not know their left hand from their right?' In that passage, God shows that he loves the city. We love the city, and believe God wants us to love and serve the city, so that is why we named it Jonah's Call."

---

[57] Timothy Keller, "A New Kind of Urban Christian: As the City Goes, so the Culture Goes," Christianity Today, 2006, http://www.allsoulsseattle.org/resources_files/A_New_Kind_of_Urban_Christian.pdf.

After a vigorous discussion about the validity of Christianity versus atheism – which ended with me pointing out that if I am wrong I lose nothing, but if I am right I gain it all – he said rather honestly, "And if I am right I gain nothing, but if I am wrong, I am screwed." He followed up with this: "I know we disagree about a lot, but I like you because you love this city and so do I. If my therapist doesn't work out, I might just try out your church."

In my view, this is common grace for the common good in action. In a post-Christendom world, our mission and ministry endeavors might include slow work with hidden results. But it is a strategy that many of us are using as we contribute to God's kingdom. As Abraham Kuyper has said:

> God is glorified in the total development toward which human life and power over nature gradually march on under the guardianship of "common grace." It is his created order, his work that unfolds here. It was he who seeded the field of humanity with all these powers. Without common grace the seed which lay hidden in that field would never have come up and blossomed. Thanks to common grace, it germinated, burgeoned, shot up high and will one day be in full flower, to reward not man but the heavenly Farmer ... A finished world will glorify God as builder and supreme Craftsman. What paradise was in bud will appear in full bloom.[58]

What's Happening in Your Church?

- Is serving the common good of the city upheld in your church as a worshipful act? And if so, how have you found ways to celebrate instances where the common good is served?
- Does your vision and mission include a strategy that allows your church to seek the welfare of the city?

4. Define Work Biblically

In Genesis 2, we get our first picture of work. It takes place in a garden, but by the time we get to Genesis 4, the picture includes a city. Genesis 2:15 says, "The Lord God took the man and put him in the Garden of Eden to work it and take care of it." In preaching on this passage, Keller offers a helpful definition of work. He says, "Work is rearranging the raw material of a particular domain for the flourishing of everyone."[59] Hence, the gardener rearranges plant life; the housewife, domestic life; the musician, sound; the janitor, waste; the lawyer, problems; and the teacher,

---

[58] Abraham Kuyper, "Abraham Kuyper: A Centennial Reader," ed. James D. Bratt (Grand Rapids: W.B. Eerdmans Publishing Co., 1998), 180-181.

[59] Quote from Tim Keller's sermon, "The Garden of God" (Genesis 2:4-17), December 2008. To hear the quote in context, go to: http://www.youtube.com/watch?v=HfTdMAoleMo.

truth. If we offer work that brings flourishing, it is good work; if we do good work to God's glory, it becomes worshipful work.

In Genesis 2, we see only good work. But by the time we leave the Garden and enter a fallen world, we begin to see bad work. Yet we do not see work itself become bad – only frustrating, requiring extra patience and toil due to the sin that separates us from God, one another, and the rest of the created order. Cain kills Abel, and Lamech writes a song celebrating death and violence. Since the Fall, we struggle with our work. At its core, however, work is still a good endeavor that is intended to produce flourishing. And, both because of God's common grace and because God is bringing lasting renewal through his redeemed people, good work still continues to take place to bring flourishing and eventual *shalom*, or total completeness in all spheres of life.[60] Hence, we now live in a world in which good work consists of rearranging raw material to bring flourishing to everyone, while bad work either fails to rearrange raw material or rearranges raw material in a way that diminishes human flourishing.

Dorothy Sayers comments on good and bad work within the church in a way that is both convicting and instructive. Sayers says:

> How can anyone remain interested in a religion which seems to have no concern with nine-tenths of life? The Church's approach to an intelligent carpenter is usually confined to exhorting him not to be drunk and disorderly in his leisure hours, and to come to church on Sundays. What the Church should be telling him is this: that the very first demand that his religion makes upon him is that he should make good tables. Church by all means, and decent forms of amusement, certainly – but what use is all that if in the very center of his life and occupation he is insulting God with bad carpentry? No crooked legs or ill-fitting drawers ever, I dare swear, came out of the carpenters shop at Nazareth.[61]

Within the nature of work, we also see that good work is primarily about contribution that leads to compensation. This compensation may or may not include money. Hence, when we do good work, contribution precedes compensation.[62]

With a proper understanding of work, pastors and teachers can commend the value of play for children who are actually doing work appropriate to their stage of development. This perspective upholds the value of motherhood, vacuuming,

---

[60] From the Hebrew שָׁלוֹם meaning completeness, soundness, welfare, and peace encompassing the whole of life.

[61] Dorothy Sayers, "Why Work?" (1942) in David S. Dockery, ed., "Faith and Learning: A Handbook for Christian Higher Education" (Nashville: B&H Publishing Group, 2012).

[62] Stephen Grabill, director of programs at The Acton Institute, has said that in good work "contribution precedes remuneration."

mowing the lawn, and doing menial tasks in our careers, as well as being a minister, a lawyer, a radiologist, or a plumber. This is vital, since our culture is often trapped by a mentality that work is either just a paycheck, or only has value if you are winning American Idol or doing brain surgery.

What's Happening in Your Church?
- In what tangible ways does your church honor workers, from janitors to doctors, when they do good work based upon the biblical definition offered in Genesis?
- When people seek to become members of your church, do you collect information on their vocations and occupations in addition to name, address, and baptism information?

5. Live Out God's Four-Fold Pattern of the Gospel
Revelation 21-22 gives us a full-color glimpse into God's final work of restoration and consummation at the end of our time. In Revelation 21:4-5, John writes:

> … "He will wipe every tear from their eyes. There will be no more death or mourning or crying or pain, for the old order of things has passed away." He who was seated on the throne said, "I am making everything new!" Then he said, "Write this down, for these words are trustworthy and true." He said to me: "It is done. I am the Alpha and the Omega, the Beginning and the End."

Faithful Christians have some differences over eschatology – you may have noticed – but we all agree that in our eternal state, we will be resurrected in the body and live in a physical world. Paul says this is a non-negotiable element of Christian faith (1 Corinthians 15). This doctrine, which we all share across our eschatological differences, has enormous implications. The new heaven and the new earth are the culmination of what Amy Sherman describes as "the big gospel," giving us a view of heaven and earth as God always intended them to be because they have such great value to him. God will not simply discard the world as a thing worn out and without value, leaving us to float forever in a dreamy otherworld that is completely disconnected to what God has made and declared to be very good. The big gospel pattern includes the good creation, the devastating Fall, the glorious redemption of man, and the restoration or consummation of all things.

Why is this so important? In my experience, when we only emphasize Creation, Fall, and Redemption, we risk leading people to conclude that God's only goal for our lives is to help us to see his goodness, our sin, and his love … and to wait until we die to finally get relief from this broken world. This view is incomplete because it ignores the overwhelming message of Jesus and the Apostles that the Kingdom, or way, of God includes the restoration of the world *beginning now* through the work of Christ and its fruits in us, and reaching its consummation at the end of this age. We call this unfolding work the "already and not yet" of God's kingdom. When pastors and teachers implement a four-fold gospel, or the big gospel, into the life of the church, great things can happen. Sherman, in an interview about her book "Kingdom Calling," describes the big gospel and its implications in this way:

> The big Gospel reminds us of God's big story. He created a paradise and invited us to steward it, legitimating all kinds of work. We blew it, but God did not retract the cultural mandate from us even after the Fall. But the Fall meant that our work would be much more difficult and sometimes feel futile. Jesus' redemption means that the restoration project is underway. Jesus' great salvation work pushes back every aspect of the curse: redeeming the broken relationship between humans and God, humans and themselves, humans with one another, and humans with the creation itself. All of that is Jesus' work, not just "saving souls." And the doctrine of consummation reminds us that King Jesus will indeed renew all things and that the eternal life we're going to live will be lived in redeemed bodies on a new Earth. So it's not going to be about being disembodied souls floating about on clouds playing harps forever and ever!
>
> When we take all that orthodoxy seriously, we see that all of our work – as farmers and teachers and architects and scientists and plumbers and bureaucrats and auto mechanics and secretaries and lawyers and cops and you-name-it – matters to God and participates in His work. We participate in His ongoing, sustaining work of creation. We participate in His work to restrain evil and corruption. We participate in His work of renewal. All our work has dignity; there is no hierarchy of "spiritual" work that is superior. And, according to the doctrine of the consummation, we can find deep meaning and purpose in our work because some of it will actually last into eternity.[63]

The church I pastor shares a massive space with multiple ministries. Because of this, I interact with people from different denominations and with differing theologies. One day, I entered the kitchen of our church and greeted a caterer who rents this space for his side business. We began to chat, and before long, our time became quite meaningful as we talked about our work and its challenges. "Jack" said to me in a voice seeking consolation:

> Pastor Jay, sometimes I feel guilty about making all this beautiful food because I know that in order for Jesus to come back – and I do want him to return – the world is just going to have to keep getting worse. And, well,

---

[63] Joe Gorra, "Vocational Stewardship: An Interview with Amy Sherman," Evangelical Philosophical Society," June 2012, http://blog.epsociety.org/2012/06/vocational-stewardship-interview-with.html.

I feel that this job making gourmet food just makes the world better, not worse. It's hard for me to figure all this stuff out.

Jack's comment staggered me because he is known in our city as a great chef, is highly sought after for the good work he does, and has even started a very successful restaurant. But his home church emphasizes that people should seek salvation by praying for Jesus to enter their hearts, and then wait for salvation to be completed by praying for God to return. Within this view, we do not have any real work to do "in the middle," except to get other people to pray these two prayers: save me, and save me again.

If you are a chef called by God to bring *shalom* (flourishing or wholeness) to the world through cooking, but you do not understand that Creation, Fall, and Redemption are followed by our cooperation with Christ's work in restoration, 90 percent of your life could actually appear as if it were opposed to the work of God! How much better is it to proclaim that being a Christian cook means that you are cooperating with Jesus, rearranging the raw materials of God's bounty in service to others as a vital act of daily worship? How much better is it for Jack to be able to pray souls into eternity while he spends 90 percent of his life practicing what we will all do for eternity – good work? Much better!

What's Happening in Your Church?

- Some churches take the stance that the only thing that matters is saving souls. To what extent do you agree or disagree with this perspective, and why?
- In what ways has your church adopted a big gospel of Creation, Fall, Redemption, and restoration/consummation in its liturgy, preaching, mission budget, and the stories it tells about God's renewal of all things?

6. Instilling Worship in All Things

In 1 Corinthians 10:31, Paul gives us an all-encompassing view of worship. He says, "So whether you eat or drink or whatever you do, do it all for the glory of God." When I accepted Christ as my Lord and Savior at the age of 14, I became immersed in a fundamentalist church, not knowing the distinction between any of the denominations or their peculiarities. Mine was a radical conversion. I was a creative teenager with a propensity for punk rock and a love for what would become known as extreme sports. Months after my conversion, while newly enrolled in a very strict Christian school, I discovered Bible memorization. I recall sitting on the edge of a skateboard ramp on my BMX bike in the fall of 1981, rehearsing the verse assigned for our ninth grade Bible class. I said, "Whatever you do, do it to the glory of God," before rolling onto the ramp. As I rode my bike, I repeated the phrase until it was memorized. It is still with me today.

However, the meaning of this verse was lost to me at the time. I recall asking God, "How can I BMX to your glory? Do I pedal like a preacher? Do I hit jumps in a religious way?"

I could not understand this verse primarily because I could only equate worship with being in church or explicitly speaking about God. Thankfully, God worked in my heart and mind over the years to develop an understanding that has allowed me to see the whole of my life as an act of worship. How? To put it succinctly, the key was a proper theology of work and rest coupled with a distinction between corporate and individual worship.

If Christians see work as a worshipful act, while also seeing Sabbath-keeping as a way of offering our rest to God, a very large part of our life becomes worship. Moreover, when we realize that God desires us to gather for corporate worship (on Sunday, for instance) and then scatter throughout the world in an offering of individual worship, the only time worship is not taking place is in our sleep! And if one prays before going to bed and invites the Lord into one's dreams, I see no reason why we cannot argue that the whole of our lives can be offered to God in worship. As Paul says, "So whether you eat or drink or whatever you do, do it all for the glory of God" (1 Corinthians 10:31).

At Jonah's Call, we identify the person we pay to lead songs on Sunday as the director of music, not the "worship leader." We have been purposeful about this because we do not want to send a message to our congregation that implies that the only time they worship is when they gather on Sunday. Instead, we are intentional about using phrases like "corporate worship" for Sunday and "individual worship" for the rest of the week. In fact, our vision statement explicitly states the same:

> Worshipping God – The transforming power of the Gospel (God generously pours out His love for us in the redemptive work of Christ who gives all of himself for all of the world) is so beautiful that it compels us to respond by offering all of our life as worship unto Him. Therefore, in corporate worship our sinful hearts are converted and our life together is restored as we hear transformational Gospel sermons, receive the sacraments, sing and pray together, and develop relationships through generous hospitality. Further, in our daily individual worship, our relationship with God is renewed and the world around us is restored as we devote ourselves to God's Word, offer Him our prayers, and live out the Gospel in every area of our lives.[64]

When we stress worship in our work and rest as a corporate and individual offering to God, Christians will be able to more vigorously live lives that are free from a fact-value split or a sacred-secular divide.

---

[64] "Vision," Jonah's Call, http://jonahscall.org/content/vision.

What's Happening in Your Church?
- Is your church's understanding of "worship" limited to what goes on in church on Sunday mornings?
- In what ways does your church include various professions and businesses in its prayer life as a congregation?

7. Being Stewards in All Aspects of Life

In 2 Kings 5, we read the story of Naaman, a great political and military leader from Aram (central Syria) who suffered from leprosy. Hearing that there was a prophet in Israel who could heal him, he loaded carriages with gold and riches and headed off to Israel, a place and people he and his countrymen disdained.

When Naaman presented himself to the prophet, Elisha saw through his leprosy to the true problem of his life: his heart. Naaman suffered from pride and self-reliance, seeking to prove himself apart from the grace and mercy of God. We know this because when Elisha told Naaman to wash seven times in the Jordan River, a river that Naaman thought to be inferior to the rivers of his country, he was clearly offended:

> "I thought that he would surely come out to me and stand and call on the name of the Lord his God, wave his hand over the spot and cure me of my leprosy. Are not Abana and Pharpar, the rivers of Damascus, better than all the waters of Israel? Couldn't I wash in them and be cleansed?" So he turned and went off in a rage (2 Kings 5:11-12).

Why the rage? Naaman was a religious person who expected that he would have to accomplish something in order to be healed. Instead, he has to prove his humility and recognize his weakness in order to be whole and saved. In 2 Kings 5:13-14, Naaman responds to the exhortation of his slaves:

> "My father, if the prophet had told you to do some great thing, would you not have done it? How much more, then, when he tells you, 'Wash and be cleansed'!" So he went down and dipped himself in the Jordan seven times, as the man of God had told him, and his flesh was restored and became clean like that of a young boy.

Similarly, in one of Disney's blockbuster installments, "Oz: The Great and Powerful" (based on "The Wizard of Oz"), we find Oz, a character very similar to Naaman. Oz is a deceitful magician from Kansas on a quest to find himself. In the film he says, "There are a lot of good men in Kansas. I don't want to be a good man. I want to be a great one." Upon facing death in the midst of a tornado, he cries out, "I don't want to die. I haven't accomplished anything yet!" To prove his greatness, he has to do the impossible: kill the wicked witch who ruthlessly rules the land. It is actually just the retelling of the ancient story of religion. Prove yourself to be great, and you will be rewarded.

According to the story of the gospel, our Naaman-like, self-imposed quest for greatness is not what makes us whole. Instead, our wholeness comes through being creatures healed by God's grace and thus bent toward conforming to his will. Sometimes that means stacking chairs, washing dishes, intentionally following rules, faithfully commuting, or lovingly changing diapers. Before we can do "great things for God," we must learn to be faithful in the little things. The gospel makes us good in order to make us great.

Though it is not explicit, the story of Naaman is about finding ourselves by stewarding little things rather than chasing "greatness." What if we shifted our emphasis from "killing the wicked witch" to turning our eyes to God and realizing that he has already given us everything we need? He has saved us by grace and wants us to use what we have to bring *shalom* to a fragmented and sick world within our respective spheres of influence.

To do this, we must begin to see ourselves as stewards, those responsible for taking care of the master's house. Stewards look at what has been given to them and seek ways to use their resources to benefit the master's house. At the end of Naaman's story in 2 Kings, we find Naaman going home with a wheelbarrow of dirt from Israel so that when he has to kneel down in a pagan temple, he might do so on the soil from which he was saved. In the end, Naaman has become a humble steward, caring for his Father's house by discovering new ways to be more faithful in his work.

When we consider stewardship as being faithful to God in the small things, our view expands far beyond money and into every sphere of life.

The great theologian Calvin Seerveld, in his book "Rainbows for the Fallen World: Aesthetic Life and Artistic Task," gives us a beautiful glimpse into an area of stewardship that is often, sadly, overlooked in the church. Though Seerveld is certainly concerned with how we steward our investments and the environment, he is also interested in how we steward our aesthetic lives – how we dress, decorate, tell stories, and play. Seerveld says:

> If we were to always drink coffee in Styrofoam cups, it would show, relatively again, where our heart is aesthetically. The Christian's concern, once saved, has usually been the fundamental one of giving those in need a cup of cold water, not bothering what we serve it in. But I'm interested also in what we middle-class people use to serve that cold water – a cool pewter mug, fine

glass, cupped hands or paper cup. Or do you let your neighbor lick it off the faucet like a Siamese cat?[65]

Challenging our notion of what constitutes a talent, Seerveld goes on to say, "I know the Lord shall save some without a cultural deed to their name, as if by fire, but God forbid that any of the little believing ones should be caught stumbling or napping when He returns, with their talent of aesthetic life tucked away, wrapped up in a hole in the ground."[66]

What's Happening in Your Church?

- How often does your church offer sermons that include the stewardship of a full economy of life (time, relationships, emotions, money, the poor, the wealthy, art, and fashion)?
- To what extent is the creation of wealth upheld in positive ways that support a robust understanding of God's desire for us to bring flourishing into the world?

8. Responding to God's Calling in All of Our Work

The call of God is so vast in Scripture that it is hard to read a passage without seeing his call to repentance, obedience, faithfulness, evangelism, and even discipline and suffering. In Ephesians 4:1-6, Paul issues a universal call to all who belong to God. He says:

As a prisoner for the Lord, then, I urge you to live a life worthy of the calling you have received. Be completely humble and gentle; be patient, bearing with one another in love. Make every effort to keep the unity of the Spirit through the bond of peace. There is one body and one Spirit, just as you were called to one hope when you were called; one Lord, one faith, one baptism; one God and Father of all, who is over all and through all and in all.

One of the most troubling aspects of calling in the church today is the failure to distinguish between God's unique call, particular call, and universal call. Many approach calling in a kind of romantic, even mystical way by asking the question, "What is God asking me to do with my life?" as if the answer is somewhere beyond a rainbow. But a more thorough look at the whole of Scripture shows us that God is calling all of us to some very practical and universal ways of living.

The universal calling of a Christian comes from the realization that there are some stewardship responsibilities God expects from everyone he created. One of the immediate joys of becoming a Christian is the ability, through the work of the Holy

---

[65] Calvin G. Seerveld, "Rainbows for the Fallen World: Aesthetic Life and Artistic Task" (Toronto: Toronto Tuppence Press, 1980).

[66] Ibid.

Spirit, to begin to fulfill some of these callings. We are all called to be citizens and members of families and of churches. Likewise, we are all called to be friends to others, to love, to be fruitful, and to multiply. Paul's appeal to the church in Ephesus was not hard to understand. It was a universal call to follow in the way of Christ. Thus, within our universal calling, being a thoughtful neighbor, a kind driver, a faithful citizen, and one who produces good work *is* God's call on my life. Though our culture stresses having an endless supply of choices in order for us to have true freedom in life, God's universal call simply lays out some very common and very basic expectations that we must obey if we are to experience the life God has called us to live. Os Guinness, in his classic book "The Call," makes the matter clear:

> Thus, for followers of Christ, calling neutralizes the fundamental position of choice in modern life. "I have chosen you," Jesus said, "you have not chosen me." We are not our own; we have been bought with a price. We have no rights, only responsibilities. Following Christ is not our initiative, merely our response, in obedience. Nothing works better to debunk the pretensions of choice than a conviction of calling. Once we have been called, we literally "have no choice."[67]

By contrast, our particular callings come from the things God has blessed us with beyond the universal calling of all mankind. Being a resident of Pittsburgh is particular to me and to many with whom I live and work, but not to all people everywhere. Moreover, some of us are in stages of life that involve being single, married, parents, or grandparents. We all have particular friends, particular jobs and vocations, incomes and resources.

Finally, there are callings that are unique to each of us. For instance, lots of people can be friends with my wife and children, but only I can sacrificially love and serve my wife Catherine, or be a father to Emma and Lydia in the unique way God has called me to. Whether it is in our job this week, or our marriage, church, household, or city, there are things in our lives that are unique, and therefore allow us to be "called for such a time as this." I believe that I presently serve as the founding pastor and rector of Jonah's Call Anglican for a unique purpose. There are folks in your life, resources you possess, and opportunities before you that are unique to you. Only you can provide flourishing to your church, household, neighborhood, company, family situation, etc., in these unique ways. Whatever aspects of your life God has afforded you, you are called to steward them, and God gives you the grace to do it! You can use them today to bring *shalom* to God's world.

I recently spoke to an entrepreneur who took a hot air popcorn popper on a trip to South America. In the city he visited, few people had ever eaten popcorn. In

---

[67] Guinness, "The Call," 167.

raising money for an orphanage there, he sold five pounds of popped corn kernels in one weekend. Excited by the possibility of this Kingdom venture, he returned with a $30 kettle corn machine and taught a team of workers from the orphanage how to make popcorn. They made the equivalent of $3,000 in three days, and he expects that the orphanage will be able to net the equivalent of $30,000 from this new business within a year, in addition to giving jobs to people who were formerly out of work. He said that God used him to take $30 (the cost of the hot air popper) and turn it into $30,000. What do you have that is particular to your own life situation (knowledge, influence, kindness, time, resources) that could be used to bring *shalom* to the particular situation you are in today?

The degree to which pastors and teachers can help their congregants see that God's call applies to universal, particular, and unique aspects of everyday life, rather than some mythic journey beyond our reach, will determine the degree to which we help a culture obsessed with choice, rather than faithfulness, to live into the call God has proclaimed to humankind.

What's Happening in Your Church?
- In what ways might your Sunday school teachers or nursery caregivers teach or model play as a legitimate calling for toddlers and children?
- How can your church shift its youth group focus to encourage teens to move from being consumers to being people universally, particularly, and uniquely called to be faithful to God's will for their lives?

9. Participating in God's Mission to Save the World

In John 20:21-22, we see clearly that God's mission to save the world has bloomed through the life, death, and resurrection of Jesus Christ. As Jesus appears in his resurrection body, he says to his disciples, " 'Peace be with you! As the Father has sent me, I am sending you.' And with that he breathed on them and said, 'Receive the Holy Spirit.' "

In the past 50 years, a movement has been afoot in the world of missions. From Leslie Newbigen to Darrell Guder, missiologists are making it clear that missionary activity is rooted in the very nature of a missionary God. Guder explains that:

> We have come to see that mission is not merely an activity of the church. Rather, mission is the result of God's initiative, rooted in God's purposes to restore and heal creation. "Mission" means "sending," and it is the central biblical theme describing the purpose of God's action in human history ... We have begun to learn that the biblical message is more radical, more inclusive, more transforming than we have allowed it to be. In particular, we have begun to see that the church of Jesus Christ is not the purpose or

goal of the gospel, but rather its instrument and witness ... God's mission is calling and sending us, the church of Jesus Christ, to be a missionary church in our own societies, in the cultures in which we find ourselves.[68]

This very robust view of mission, rooted in God's desire to restore and heal the world, is known as the *missio Dei*, or the mission of God. Of course, it includes the saving of souls; that will always be central to the task of the church. But carrying out the *missio Dei* also includes learning to be good stewards of the earth, from architecture and neighborhoods, to mothering and being good sportsmen.

I recall interviewing David Greusel, one of the chief architects that created Pittsburgh's renowned PNC Park. As we sat and talked over dinner in downtown Pittsburgh, David told me about his longing to find meaning in his work and the deep call he felt to serve God as an architect. As we ate and talked, David pointed out a multi-storied grey building across the street. "The men who made that building believed that there was no meaning in the world, no God, no everlasting life." He went on to say, "And now people have to suffer with the results of those beliefs as they walk through dreary halls and stare at cold walls. As architects, we shape life by building structures, and then those structures shape us." It occurred to me as we spoke how, as a Christian architect, David clearly saw his role as one sent on a mission from God to bring restoration and healing to the created order.

Unfortunately, many within the walls of the church, including pastors, fail to see that the work of the scattered church includes both saving souls and creating high-rises. Steven Garber, president of the Washington Institute for Faith, Vocation & Culture, gives us painful examples of this failure in his afterward to Amy Sherman's book, "Kingdom Calling." Garber says:

> [Most Christian people] spend their lives in the marketplace of the world, hoping [that] there is some honest connection between what they do and the work of God in the world. They yearn to see their vocations as integral, not incidental, to the missio Dei ... One man I talked with this past year told me something of his life. For decades he has labored away in the business world, working hard, taking up increasingly complex tasks that involve people and money. Over the years he has given himself with honest humility to service in the churches where he has lived, and is a kind, loyal, thoughtful man (my reading of him, not his description of himself). With some pain, he said, "I've never had the sense that the pastor thought of someone like me when he was preparing his sermon. It always feels more like he imagines that people live in the church, not the world."[69]

---

[68] Darrell L. Guder, ed., "Missional Church: A Vision for the Sending of the Church in North America" (Grand Rapids: Wm. B. Eerdmans Publishing Co., 1998), 4-5.

[69] Steven Garber, afterward to "Kingdom Calling: Vocational Stewardship for the Common Good," by Amy Sherman (Downers Grove: InterVarsity Press, 2011).

In his 2001 Q Talk on vocation, Garber drives home the need for a more robust understanding of mission in relation to vocation:

> We must commit to a theological imagination that makes sense of who we are and how we are to live, especially to understanding the meaning of vocation as integral, not incidental, to the missio Dei. We need a theological imagination that is rich and true enough to push back away from every sort of dualism, from every effort to privilege the sacred over the secular, the not-for-profit over the profit, of saving grace over common grace. The paradigm has to change, and we need the theological grist running through the mills of our minds that is able to do that ... When was the last time that architects and builders, teachers and librarians, doctors and nurses, artists and journalists, lawyers and judges, were prayed for in your congregation? We could do that, you know? We need to keep praying for the Young Life staff people, and the Wycliffe Bible Translators, but we also need to pray for the butchers and bakers and candlestick-makers too, remembering that most of what God is doing in the world is being done in and through the vocations of his people.[70]

What's Happening in Your Church?

- In what ways does your church tell stories that highlight the work of the gospel in a variety of vocations (janitor, missionary, and CEO)?

- How often does your church hear sermons that explicitly talk about the marketplace and domestic vocation?

10. Being a Church With a Vocationally Infused Vision and Mission

Revelation 21:22-27 gives us a glimpse into God's consummation of the work he will do when the cosmos is healed and restored. John writes:

> I did not see a temple in the city, because the Lord God Almighty and the Lamb are its temple. The city does not need the sun or the moon to shine on it, for the glory of God gives it light, and the Lamb is its lamp. The nations will walk by its light, and the kings of the earth will bring their splendor into it. On no day will its gates ever be shut, for there will be no night there. The glory and honor of the nations will be brought into it. Nothing impure will ever enter it, nor will anyone who does what is shameful or deceitful, but only those whose names are written in the Lamb's book of life.

---

[70] Steven Garber, "Vocation as Intergral, Not Incidental" (The Washington Institute for Faith, Vocation & Culture, April 2011), http://www.washingtoninst.org/893/vocation-as-integral-not-incidental/.

My wife and I attended Redeemer Presbyterian in the early 1990s when it was only a church plant meeting in the afternoon in a Unitarian church building on Manhattan's Upper East Side. In those early days, Keller was not yet a best-selling author, but a bookish type who could quote full sections of the writings of C.S. Lewis and J.R.R. Tolkien by heart and who gave, for some, too many sermon illustrations from episodes of Star Trek. Even then, however, Keller always put forth a vision of Redeemer being a church that loved the city. In fact, over the 20 years that I have attentively followed his preaching, I cannot count the number of times he has held up a vision of Redeemer that seeks the welfare of the city. It is literally part of Redeemer's vision:

> As a church of Jesus Christ, Redeemer exists to help build a great city for all people through a movement of the gospel that brings personal conversion, community formation, justice, and cultural renewal to New York City and, through it, the world.[71]

When churches have a great vision to become a place of salt and light with a big gospel and biblical view of work, mission, and calling, they more effectively form life-giving habits while breaking those that fragment the Word of God and the ways of God.

A very quick look at the vision statements of churches where thought leaders attend is telling.

Tom Nelson, author of "Work Matters" and pastor of Christ Community Church in suburban Kansas City, offers this vision: "A caring family of multiplying disciples, influencing our community and world for Jesus Christ."[72] The Falls Church Anglican, led by John Yates and church home of Steve Garber, has embedded in their vision and mission a clear sense of place, calling, and renewal:

Where We Are Placed:

- In the Nation's Capital – we have a significant responsibility and the potential for vital Christian influence.

What We Are Called to:

- Live Out God's Word in Our Whole Lives – we seek to know and apply Biblical truth in our church life, our family life, through our work, and by serving God wherever we are.

---

[71] "Visions and Values," Redeemer Presbyterian Church, http://www.redeemer.com/learn/about_us/vision_and_values.

[72] "About Christ Community," Christ Community Church Website, http://www.ccefc.org/about#what-we-value-tab.

- Renew God's Church in Word and Spirit – we seek to raise up leaders from every generation for the church; to plant churches; to offer ourselves, our experience and our facilities as resources to the wider church.[73]

At Jonah's Call, we have worked hard to craft a vision statement that upholds a view of the church that is both salty and full of light. This work has helped us build consensus among leaders, as well as disciple our congregation in key teachings and behaviors around a view of the church that loves the city and seeks its renewal. We do this while upholding the church as a holy place set apart to preserve God's Word, and an institution that both shapes and is shaped by culture. Our vision is: Joining in a Gospel Movement that brings flourishing to the city as we worship God, love our neighbors and shape culture.

Embedded in our vision and mission is a whole-life description of renewal:

> Loving Our Neighbors – The inclusivity of the Gospel (God fully accepts us as his children because of the atoning work of Christ on the cross) is so intimate that it restores our ability to know and be known by our neighbors. Therefore, we seek to be a church that offers forgiveness to those who have harmed us, sacrificial love to everyone we encounter, and generous hospitality to all who come into our homes, work places and church. As a Church, we strive to live out our life together by offering permanence to transients, deep roots to established families and belonging in worship and service to others.

Additionally, we have explicitly stated in our vision that we seek to shape culture and explain the implications for the church:

> Shaping Culture – The regenerative nature of the Gospel (God is actively engaged in renewing every square inch of our world from the way it is to the way it is intended to be) is so pervasive that it makes every aspect of our daily life an important part of God's renewal of all things. Therefore, both corporately and individually, Jonah's Call is passionate about partnering with others to bring about justice to the oppressed, cultural renewal to our city, and beauty to God's creation.

Of course, we are all capable of failing to line up our actions with our vision. But the work of casting a vision of a preferred tomorrow is a major step for any church that is seeking to break bad habits like a sacred-secular divide and a fact-value split.

---

[73] "Vision, Values, Mission, & Ministries," The Falls Church Anglican, 2012, http://www.tfcanglican.org/pages/page.asp?page_id=222265.

What's Happening in Your Church?

- Is your church's vision and mission statement used to form the programs, practices, and habits that form your church identity?

- In what ways does your church's vision capture a four-fold gospel and include a concern for the community?

Conclusion

These aspirations for reform may seem daunting. But the local church is a community created and sustained by God's grace, and we can continue to rely on that grace. The church is still the hope of the world. If we take on this great task, the Lord will not fail to bless us, or to accomplish his purposes in the world.

Made for
COMMUNITY

David Wright

It is not good for man to be alone! We are made for relationship and community, and our social nature defines the world of work. All our work is done with others and for others, through the vast web of relationships that we call "the economy." We are all embedded in this great moral system of exchange at every moment of our lives as we buy and sell, hire and work, build and invest. As David Wright shows in this excerpt from the book "How God Makes the World a Better Place," the church once addressed economic realities and must do so again today. Wright explores how the Wesleyan movement played a critical role in the development of the Industrial Revolution, both constructively (affirming that factory jobs were good, honest labor that served God and the community) and critically (challenging abuses and injustices as they emerged). He shares his experiences in Haiti, showing that what is most needed to alleviate poverty is not an outpouring of money, but a new outpouring of moral vision that affirms the rights of the poor to work, own, save, and participate in the modern economy.

David Wright is the president of Indiana Wesleyan University in Marion, Ind. He grew up in the Philippines as the son of missionaries, and later served as field coordinator for the Wesleyan Church's mission efforts in Haiti in the 1980s. Wright has been working in Christian higher education in the United States since then; he holds a Ph.D. in philosophy from the University of Kentucky. He is also an active pilot with his own plane. If you like this excerpt, check out the full book "How God Makes the World a Better Place," which introduces the full integration of faith with the world of work and economics from a Wesleyan perspective.

The Gospel of Christ knows of no religion, but social; no holiness but social holiness.
- John Wesley

One of the most enduring principles of the global Wesleyan movement grew from John Wesley's deep conviction that there is no such thing as solitary religion.

One of his most famous statements is this one: " 'Holy solitaries' is a phrase no more consistent with the gospel than holy adulterers."

He went further:

> The Gospel of Christ knows of no religion, but social; no holiness but social holiness. Faith working by love is the length and breadth and depth of Christian perfection. This commandment we have from Christ that he who loves God, must love his brother also ... [We must] manifest our love by doing good unto all ... especially to them that are of the household of faith.[74]

Through his teaching and his actions, John Wesley ensured that this conviction became one of the strongest identifying characteristics of the Wesleyan movement. Christians discipled in this movement were, and are, called to work in ways that promote community well-being.

Our spiritual heritage teaches us that our discipleship of personal spiritual growth actually has its application in the discipleship of community service. Wesleyans, when they are most faithful to their roots, are committed to understanding what makes communities healthy. They are committed to create and run institutions, businesses, and organizations that make communities healthy places. They engage in the public work that creates and sustains healthy communities. Wesleyans are called to work that promotes community well-being.

The Wesleyan Movement and the Cornish Mining Industry

We don't have space here to do more than give a couple of examples of how this principle worked itself out in the Wesleyan movement of Wesley's day. One of the most intriguing examples is the way that the movement made its impact on the metal mining communities of Cornwall in the south of England.

The Cornish Mining World Heritage Site, while not a religious organization, pays tribute on their website to the way that the Wesleyan movement made Cornish mining communities better places.

> Methodism spoke to the Cornish people in a language they could understand and helped them to make sense of a rapidly changing world.

---

[74] John Wesley and Charles Wesley, preface to "Hymns and Sacred Poems" (London: W. Strahan, 1739), v-vi.

Chapels became the hub of the community in most Cornish mining towns and villages, bringing people together for social events as well as services.[75]

The Wesleyan movement, because it engaged common people in their own language, at their own locations, and addressed the actual pressing issues they were facing, wove itself into the fabric of local communities. This gave hope to people who faced seemingly overwhelming circumstances that seemed far beyond their power to control.

> Methodism was very much a community faith; meetings were held in cottages and barns which made services easily accessible and ideally suited to the close-knit societies that were formed around Cornish metal mining. The domestic setting helped integrate spirituality and rationality with Cornish indigenous folk beliefs. ...
>
> This important message brought comfort, hope and security to a population that faced daily dangers in the hazardous environment of metal mines and increasing uncertainty in a world being rapidly reshaped by industrialisation.[76]

The Wesleyan movement made these communities better simply by creating networks and links for communication, analysis, accountability, and action. It was a movement centered in the connections between people. People felt included. They were enabled to take ownership of their lives, their families, and their communities.

> These small groups of early Methodists were closely bound together by a word-of-mouth network and the constant movements of itinerants and lay preachers, who were able to travel and interact with different communities in ways that would have been near impossible for the Anglican clergy, who were tied to the church building itself. The use of charismatic lay preachers, like Billy Bray, who preached to the people in the dialect they spoke, gave people [a] sense of social inclusion. Huge crowds were drawn to open-air meetings, and Wesley preached to hundreds at a time in places such as Gwennap Pit.[77]

One of the most interesting factors illustrated by the Cornish mining communities was the connection between the Wesleyan movement and the mining businesses themselves. The movement did not oppose the businesses. Instead, it engaged both the business and the people who worked in them. The Wesleyan message, meetings, and organizations gave confidence to the people working in the businesses, and helped those who led the businesses to do so in ways that made their communities more healthy.

---

[75] "Religion," Cornish Mining World Heritage, http://www.cornish-mining.org.uk/delving-deeper/religion.
[76] Ibid.
[77] Ibid.

The link between mining and Methodism was strengthened by the role played by the newly emerging entrepreneurial and merchant class, which was becoming particularly conspicuous where the influence of the Anglican Church was already in decline. Numerous mine captains were also Methodist preachers who communicated to their communities the powerful messages of respectability and self-improvement, thus helping to ensure that Methodism became the most relevant religious institution for labourers and the working class.[78]

This is an example of one of the most enduring features of the Wesleyan view of work. Wesleyans embrace the meaningful work that is present in a community. Wesleyans find ways to create meaningful and rewarding work that helps to ensure that community needs are met.

Wesleyans and the Business of Making Communities Better through Learning

John Wesley's lifelong commitment to learning is another powerful illustration of the Wesleyan movement's commitment to community wellbeing. Wesley was himself a highly educated person. He enjoyed the best education that 18th century England could provide. He read widely all of his life. His journals show that his own intellectual interests ranged far and wide and never diminished even late in his life.

This is interesting because, unlike so many highly educated people, Wesley didn't confine his interactions to people like himself. He believed, and clearly enjoyed, moving freely and purposefully across all social and intellectual classes.

There is an interesting correspondence between John Wesley and a wealthy, highly educated woman named Miss J. C. March. She was captivated by the Wesleyan message and wanted to experience full salvation. But when Wesley told her that she would be greatly blessed and helped in this if she would visit the poor, she objected. She told him she believed that she should associate with "people of taste and good character." Wesley's response is revealing.

> I have found some of the uneducated poor who have exquisite taste and sentiment; and many, very many, of the rich who have scarcely any at all ... I want you to converse more ... with the poorest of the people, who, if they have not taste, have souls, which you may forward in their way to heaven. And they have (many of them) faith and the love of God in a larger measure than any persons I know. Creep in among these in spite of dirt and an hundred disgusting circumstances, and thus put off the gentlewoman.

---

[78] Ibid.

Do not confine your conversation to genteel and elegant people. I should like this as well as you do; but I cannot discover a precedent for it in the life of our Lord or any of His Apostles.[79]

Clearly John Wesley did not value associating with poor and uneducated people simply because this was a way he could gain the personal benefit of spiritual blessing. He spent time with people of all classes because he genuinely valued and enjoyed them. He saw, despite their difficult circumstances, the great value in people who were often pushed to the margins of society, and blamed for their own difficult circumstances.

The Wesleyan movement embraced the task of working in ways that helped people like this better themselves, and thus, better their communities. For Wesley, learning was a powerful tool in this work.

In an Isis journal article titled "John Wesley and Science in 18th Century England," history professor Robert Schofield noted the fact that movements that work with poor and less well-educated people can take on anti-intellectual tendencies. Wesley, though, would have none of this.

Wesley was disturbed lest his "Methodists" follow that pattern ... Wesley denied the criticism that Methodism taught the rejection of human learning – adding, characteristically, that learning was "highly expedient for a guide of souls" though not absolutely necessary. He insisted that "the author of our nature designed that we should not destroy but regulate our desire for knowledge"; and "It cannot be that the people will grow in grace unless they give themselves to reading. A reading people will always be a knowing people."[80]

This pursuit of learning for his great movement illustrates a couple of interesting facts about the way John Wesley viewed work that bettered the community. On the one hand, he was passionately committed to calling the members of the movement to learn. On the other hand, he did this by the entrepreneurial creation of a publishing enterprise.

It is not, therefore, surprising that Wesley took steps in support of his convictions. He encouraged schooling for all of his followers and especially for his lay-preachers. He established schools and reading classes, supervising their curricula and recommending reading lists for those schools and for those of a similar type started by others. Finally, he started his own printing plant where he printed books that he could recommend.

---

[79] "The Letters of John Wesley," Wesley Center Online, 2000, http://wesley.nnu.edu/john-wesley/the-letters-of-john-wesley/wesleys-letters-1776/.

[80] Robert E. Schofield, "John Wesley and Science in 18th Century England," Isis 44 (December 1953): 332.

As a writer, editor, publisher, and printer, he was probably not equaled by any other person in England.[81]

Wesley's publishing enterprise was enormously successful. It made Wesley very wealthy. Some estimate he earned as much as £30,000 (more than $6 million today) over his life from this highly successful entrepreneurial business. He kept none of this money for himself. All but the barest of necessities was reinvested in the work of the movement.

The point here is that this work illustrates two foundational characteristics of the Wesleyan movement and its approach to work.

First, Wesleyans engage the people of their communities, particularly those people who live on the margins. By spending time with these people, Wesleyans learn crucial aspects and gain valuable perspectives about the needs of their communities.

Second, Wesleyans embrace all kinds of creative ways to meet those needs, including by starting entrepreneurial businesses and nonprofit organizations.

In this way, Wesleyans live out their calling to do work that promotes community well-being.

Learning Wesleyan Lessons in Haiti

When I was 26, I moved to Haiti to work. It was, and remains, the most challenging personal and professional experience of my life.

Haiti stretched and taxed me in every way. Most of all, Haiti challenged my assumptions and gave me reason to dig deeply into the factors that make communities healthy and unhealthy. Haiti is where I truly learned the power of work, and the crushing effects on communities when they cannot sustain meaningful and rewarding work. Haiti is where I saw in action the organic link between the structures and ideas that lie at the heart of a community, and the ability of that community to sustain meaningful and rewarding work. Haiti was where I began to learn the reality of the Wesleyan principles of work we have been exploring here.

When I went to Haiti I was no stranger to the grimmer realities of life in the poorer communities of our world. I was born in a missionary hospital in one of the poorest neighborhoods of Manila. I grew up in small, poor villages in the rural provinces of the Philippines. I was no stranger to poverty. But Haiti seemed different somehow.

The Haitian people are a marvel of good humor and relentless hope in a world of endless vulnerability. The land is spare and beautiful, though it is ravished by

---

[81] Ibid.

ecological disasters caused by natural and human forces. Haiti has its own culture, a fascinating and vibrant blend of African, Caribbean, European, and American influences.

Not too long after we arrived, my wife and I began to experience something that we hadn't encountered before. Once we were settled in our home, a steady stream of visitors came to see us. They were almost always polite and friendly, showing genuine interest in and care for us. Our neighbors welcomed us to their country with genuine warmth. But before every conversation ended, our visitors would share a story of hardship and need, and then they would ask if we could help them. This happened so regularly we grew to expect it. This predictable turn of conversation became uncomfortable, but we did our best to respond with help where we could.

Eventually, however, I began to ask questions. Why was this so much a feature of Haitian life? I began to observe as widely and carefully as I could, given my limited knowledge at the time. Clearly most Haitians were painfully poor. But unlike the poor places of my upbringing, Haitians were not just poor in that they lacked material possessions. The deeper I looked, the more I saw my neighbors struggling with a more fundamental poverty. They lived with a desperate vulnerability to natural threats such as hunger, illness, and natural disasters. Yet even deeper, they lived with a vulnerability to political conflict and to exploitation by powerful interests.

Most Haitians lived in unstable and vulnerable houses. Their communities lacked the means to create and sustain stable transportation, communication, energy, health care, and education infrastructures. I watched them cope heroically with these vulnerabilities. And they asked for my help. In the course of time I soon realized that while many asked for specific things such as money, medicine, clothing, and food, there was one thing they asked for far more than any other. They asked for work.

My Haitian neighbors either asked if there was work they could do for me, or they asked if I could provide them with resources to start their own entrepreneurial work. I came to realize that my Haitian friends really did not want charity – not from me, not from foreign governments, not from their own government. They wanted to work. There was something natural and organic and untutored in this request. They didn't ask for work because their political ideology told them they should. They asked for work because they wanted to work.

I went to Haiti with the assumption that God somehow, in ways I had never quite discovered, rewards faithful Christians with a good standard of living. Haiti, with its many Christian poor, plainly showed me that this was not always true. I went to Haiti with the assumption that churches, communities, and countries grow strong through spiritual revivals. Haiti plainly showed me that this is true, but not quite in the way I had assumed. Though I would have denied these assumptions at the time, Haiti forced me to discover certain powerful truths inherent in my Wesleyan tradition that perhaps I already "knew," yet somehow they remained unrealized in my understanding.

I had been well prepared to teach spiritual subjects like Bible, theology, and church leadership. I had no preparation at all to understand the ways that communities work, the factors that shape healthy communities, the needs that we are called to address, and the devastating consequences of communities' inability to sustain the structures that make meaningful, rewarding work possible.

I could help Haitian Christians with spiritual factors. Yet I had no working understanding of the power of my own heritage – John Wesley's insistence that we should sit with the poor and thereby seek to understand their situation; that we should work to create structures and mechanisms that give them understanding, voice, and empowerment in shaping their communities; that we should encourage them in the creation of businesses and organizations that naturally create wealth and thus build the infrastructures that sustain healthy societies.

A powerful insight I learned by sitting with my neighbors in Haiti is that John Wesley was right about people. Haitians are bright, creative, industrious people. In my experience, although their understanding can always be improved with careful learning, poor people are aware of the broken mechanisms that keep their communities unhealthy. Left to their own devices, they will most of the time choose industry, entrepreneurialism, and personal ownership over charity and dependency.

Perhaps the most powerful insight I learned in Haiti is the absolute importance of the social systems and structures in which people live. The power of the economic and legal system either to destroy or to enable meaningful work, to decimate a community or to empower a community to thrive, simply cannot be overstated. It is a high priority for societies to protect the efficacy of the weak and the vulnerable: When their efficacy is taken away from them, they are robbed of dignity and they are institutionally prohibited from serving their fellow man and from providing for their own needs. In order for people and communities to thrive, a wide variety of business and civil institutions need to be created to solve the underlying economic and social problems.

It is beyond the scope of this [essay] to explore the nature of healthy political, legal, and economic frameworks. But Daron Acemoglu and James Robinson have provided one of the most insightful and instructive studies on the question of why some nations thrive and others struggle with pervasive poverty that seems impervious to change. These two researchers, the former an economist from MIT and the latter a political scientist and economist from Harvard, set out to discover and explain the mechanisms behind this phenomenon.

Their book, "Why Nations Fail," outlines their basic findings:

> We live in an unequal world ... In rich countries, individuals are healthier, live longer, and are much better educated. They also have access to a range of amenities and options in life, from vacations to career paths, that people in poor countries can only dream of. People in rich countries also drive on roads without potholes, and enjoy toilets, electricity and running water in their houses. They also typically have governments that do not arbitrarily arrest or harass them; on the contrary, the governments provide services, including education, health care, roads, and law and order. Notable, too, is the fact that the citizens vote in elections and have some voice in the political direction their countries take.[82]

What, they ask, explains these differences? They point out popular current theories. One theory is the "geography hypothesis," which says that "the great divide between rich and poor countries is created by geographical differences."[83] Many of the world's poor countries are in tropical climates, while many of the world's richer countries are in temperate climates. This hypothesis doesn't hold up to careful study.

Another is the "culture hypothesis," which says that national prosperity can be traced to sets of beliefs, values, and ethics, much of which rests on religious foundations.[84] Culture, they note, is important and can have an impact on the way nations develop. But culture is not an adequate explanation for why some nations develop and maintain prosperity and others remain locked in poverty.

A third popular hypothesis is the "ignorance hypothesis," which says that some countries remain poor because they and their leaders simply do not know how to manage their countries so as to produce wealth.[85] Further, the world's wealthy countries do not know how to share their knowledge appropriately. But this hypothesis does not hold up, and doesn't adequately explain why nations fail.

Acemoglu and Robinson propose an entirely different explanation that is both enlightening and encouraging.

> Countries differ in their economic success because of their different institutions, the rules influencing how the economy works, and the incentives that motivate people ... Inclusive economic institutions ... are

---

[82] Daron Acemoglu and James A. Robinson, "Why Nations Fail: The Origins of Power, Prosperity, and Poverty" (New York: Crown Publishers, 2012), 40-41.

[83] Ibid., 48.

[84] Ibid., 57.

[85] Ibid., 63-64.

those that allow and encourage participation by the great mass of people in economic activities that make best use of their talents and skills and that enable individuals to make the choices they wish. To be inclusive, economic institutions must feature secure private property, an unbiased system of law, and a provision of public services that provides a level playing field in which people can exchange and contract; it also must permit the entry of new businesses and allow people to choose their careers.[86]

Communities that provide these kinds of institutions build the foundation for well-being, because in these communities people can use their God-given creativity, talents, and hard work to create and spread value widely among themselves and their neighbors. On the other hand, communities in which such institutions are prevented from developing, or are inhibited, extract value and diminish well-being.

I saw these lessons at work firsthand in Haiti. Haiti taught me the inherent value of work and the God-given hunger that all people have to do meaningful and rewarding work. But it also taught me that this individual need to express the image of God in us through meaningful work must be placed within a fair and beneficial political, legal, and economic framework. Without a fair and dependable court system that ensured that the basic virtues of honesty, fairness, and ownership would be followed by everyone, individual Haitians struggled to turn their creativity and their hard work into value for themselves, their families, and their fellow Haitians. Without a banking system that ensured that money could be protected and that money could be borrowed on fair and workable terms to build small businesses, Haitians did not have the working capital to turn their ideas into viable businesses that could provide for their own needs and provide the goods and services their neighbors needed.

Haiti is where I began to learn the power of my own heritage and its view of work. It is where I began to see the power of systems that I had always taken for granted, even though I grew up as a missionary kid living under impoverished conditions.

At the heart of our Wesleyan heritage is a commitment to the well-being of communities and an understanding that it is in the pursuit of this wellbeing that God teaches us the most important lessons about our own spiritual maturity.

Characteristics of Healthy Communities

Before we leave this exploration of the Wesleyan commitment to community well-being, we should briefly summarize some key characteristics of healthy and unhealthy communities.

---

[86] Ibid., 73-75.

Harvard sociology professor William Julius Wilson has done extensive research in urban communities where work has disappeared. He found that all communities that cannot sustain meaningful, stable work eventually take on certain social and personal features with undesirable consequences. In communities where work disappears:

Social organization declines. Structures and activities that link members of a community together begin to disappear. Community members become isolated, retreating into cocoons of silence and disengagement. The public commons falls into disrepair.

Social integration disappears. Communities without work have less socioeconomic diversity. Healthy communities are made up of people and families of various economic, educational, and professional statuses. Role models are available for children to observe. Patterns of productive behavior are reinforced even for those who may be going through hard times. Businesses and service organizations locate in the community. But when work disappears, all of these characteristics begin to disappear, changing forever the look and essence of the community.

Community makeup changes. Businesses and service agencies move out. Schools struggle to find resources and to attract and retain top-quality teachers. The physical infrastructure falls into disrepair.

Illegitimate behavior increases. Dysfunctional, illegal, and antisocial behaviors tend to increase when work disappears from a community. In time, left unchecked, these behaviors come to define a community, feeding a spiral of violence, fear, and decay.

Personal apathy increases. As the situation worsens, those who remain in the community adopt a crippling sense of apathy. The problems seem so deep-rooted, and the solutions so unattainable, that even those who wish for something better, give up.[87]

Wilson published his research and findings listed above in "When Work Disappears: The World of the New Urban Poor." In this work he also said:

The consequences of high neighborhood joblessness are more devastating than those of high neighborhood poverty. A neighborhood in which people are poor but employed is different from a neighborhood in which people are poor and jobless. Many of today's problems in the inner-city ghetto neighborhoods – crime, family dissolution, welfare, low levels of

---

[87] William Julius Wilson, "When Work Disappears: The World of the New Urban Poor" (New York: Knopf, 1996).

social organization, and so on – are fundamentally a consequence of the disappearance of work.[88]

These are the factors we can observe the Wesleyan movement addressing in 18th century England. They are the factors that our Wesleyan commitment to community well-being should lead us to address today, no matter where they exist in the world.

Our theological heritage helps us to see that there is a connection between the ideas that lie at the heart of communities and the health of those communities. Part of our discipleship challenge is to work in ways that encourage people to embrace ideas that promote healthy communities.

What are the conditions that best allow communities to create and sustain meaningful and rewarding work? Here are four ideas that we can observe in our movement and that scholarship and experience link to healthy communities.

Virtue

Virtue is absolutely essential. In particular, there must be a certain level of trust involved in every business and organizational transaction that takes place. Whether we go to the store and hand cash to the cashier to buy groceries, or whether we put our credit card number online, there is always an element of trust. Trust is absolutely essential to the healthy functioning of communities. It is remarkable how much one can see elements in the Wesleyan movement that build networks of trust to counteract the challenges that came with the industrialization of England in the 18th century. Much of this trust is so implicit that we don't even think about it. But it is absolutely essential to the healthy functioning of communities. Trust is everywhere. A primary mechanism that communities need in order to protect the principles that build trust is the protections and provisions of law and order, proper authority, and justice.

Rule of Law

Thus, the second system that is essential in healthy communities is the rule of law. The rule of law simply means that the law will be enforced equally and fairly among all the participants regardless of any other characteristics that may apply to them. If trust is violated somehow, either by inattention or by deceit, in a healthy community neighbors can then appeal to the rule of law. If the businesses we create decide not to pay our workers, they may appeal to the law. If the customers our businesses serve refuse to pay, we may appeal to the law. In healthy communities laws are seen to be fair and applicable to all equally. When laws are passed that privilege one group over another, problems inevitably arise.

---

[88] Ibid., xiii.

Ownership Rights

Ownership rights are another essential element necessary for healthy communities. John Wesley taught the members of the Methodist movement that, ultimately, all property belongs to God. We are simply stewards of the things God has given us. Nevertheless, the movement operated on the assumption that healthy communities enshrine the principle that individuals hold and use private property responsibly, indeed, in ways in keeping with God's purpose. The Wesleyan movement worked to shape healthy communities where members worked to create wealth, use it wisely, and invest it in the greater good of the community.

Ethic of Value Creation

Societies that manage to nurture a shared ethic that honors the creation of value lay the groundwork for widespread well-being. This ethic rests ultimately on the biblical command that we are to love our neighbors as ourselves. Value creation occurs when people use their creativity, knowledge, insight, and work to create things that are of value that others need and want. This process reflects the genius of God's creation. It benefits those who do it, and it spreads benefit throughout a community. Societies that honor this principle, that provide systemic and institutional frameworks which encourage it, and that reward it appropriately lay the groundwork for community well-being.

So now, with that overview, is it possible for anyone to embody this kind of commitment to community well-being? Yes it is. Meet Keith Stanton of Christchurch, New Zealand.

I want the whole Christ for my Savior, the whole Bible for my book, the whole Church for my fellowship, and the whole world for my mission field.

– John Wesley

The Thirst Quencher

It began with planning a summer holiday in 1988. Keith Stanton of Christchurch, New Zealand, told his wife, "'I would like to go and travel to some exotic place,' and she said, 'Well, I'm not going anywhere there's not clean toilets!' " They discussed going on tour with World Vision, where their time would be spent visiting projects and sightseeing. "We decided World Vision wouldn't give us any rubbishy accommodations!" he laughed.

On that first tour the Stantons visited a village in Bangladesh where World Vision had installed a school, water supply, and sanitation system. Previously, the village of about 6,000 had been losing a majority of children before the age of five due to waterborne diseases. The women were concerned about their future, so Keith donated 50 pedal sewing machines with which they could start a business. He relayed, "Eighteen months later, we received in the mail a big parcel of clothing!"

A couple of years later, 600 people were involved in the village's worldwide export clothing business.

"From then on it was water; I was motivated really by that first story, how water changed the lives of these people in this village, and also provided the opportunity for children to grow and develop into mature adulthood." At last count, Keith has supported 346 water projects in 16 countries, mostly in Africa.

Keith's grandfather was a Methodist home missionary who went on to be a director for the China Inland Mission. But with 13 children to support, his grandfather eventually started a stationery and printing business. Keith worked there with his father, and at the age of 45, established his own business. "That's really where I got the funds from to start the projects," he explained.

"Wesley was a great encourager of people to go and to make money and to use it to help others. And that was part of the philosophy that came down through my upbringing." But there was a time when the Methodist Church in New Zealand frowned upon people who were in business. "They felt people's money was an evil thing. I don't know where that idea came from; it's not true, because without money you can't do too much to help others. I always had the feeling it was there to share, there to help."

By 2002, Keith had sold the business and decided to visit some of the projects. "I wanted to make sure the money was being well spent and was fulfilling the needs, that it would go on and serve the people for years." At the age of 78, Keith is still at it. His latest water project will provide about 14,000 people with clean water. He is also building a school in Tanzania and has funded Wesleyan Methodist church buildings.

"[Giving] is good for the receiver, and it's also good for the giver," he stated. "The satisfaction I get out of it is actually seeing the smiling faces of the children, and seeing people have the opportunity to grow and live a life of fulfillment."

Perhaps most importantly, Keith's lifelong commitment to creating viable businesses that were focused on meeting the needs of the people his business could serve was rewarded with the creation of wealth. Keith's lifelong commitment to the Wesleyan principles of discipline, self-control, and thriftiness allowed him to have resources he could give away. God used his faithfulness to bless others through two powerful means – his wonderful charitable spirit and his ability to create sustainable businesses that produce well-being for others and wealth that he could put toward good uses.

Keith's story aptly illustrates the discipleship principles embedded in the Wesleyan heritage.

REFLECTION QUESTIONS

1. Why does Wright think it is essential to the pastor's task to describe the economy in moral and spiritual terms? How can we see a need for this in our communities today?

2. Wright argues that just institutions are key to helping communities overcome poverty. What opportunities are there in your community to help change institutions in ways that will help the poor flourish? What are the limits to what we can accomplish this way?

3. Wright identifies four "social conditions" that help communities sustain work. How much are these conditions present in your community? What can you do to help cultivate them?

Made for
RESPONSIBILITY

Scott Rae

If we are made for community, we are made for responsibility. If we love others, we must avoid becoming a burden to them. So each household must strive to support itself economically through the work of its own members. Responsible people produce more than they consume. But this is not an ethic of isolated individualism; quite the contrary, we support ourselves by doing work that serves others and creates flourishing and sustainable communities. That is also an exercise of responsibility. And those who are able to support themselves are also responsible to provide for those who cannot. As Scott Rae demonstrates in this careful and thoughtful essay, an economic ethic of simultaneous *independence* and *interdependence* runs through Scripture literally from beginning to end.

Scott Rae is the dean of the faculty, a professor of Christian ethics, and the chair of the philosophy department at Biola University's Talbot School of Theology in southern California. He also serves on the national advisory committee of the Oikonomia Network. He holds a Ph.D. from the University of Southern California and is a leading Christian ethical thinker. If you like this essay, check out his two books on economic ethics – "Business for the Common Good," co-authored with Kenman Wong, and "The Virtues of Capitalism," co-authored with Austin Hill – in which he and his co-authors flesh out a Christian vision for work, business, the marketplace, and economic systems. His other books include "Doing the Right Thing" (based on Chuck Colson's video series of the same name), "Moral Choices," "Brave New Families," and "Body and Soul."

In my experience, it's not easy to get pastors to see the relevance of economics. But economic systems and practices shape our lives daily. In some cases, our economic environment helps us become more responsible – responsible for the way we live our own lives, and responsible for treating one another rightly – as God intends. In other cases, we are challenged by economic conditions and systems that make it harder for us to live as responsible beings. If we want to understand the meaning and purpose of our lives, we need to think theologically and ethically about the structures within which we live.

In this essay, I begin with the assumption that pastors already affirm the dignity of work in general, since most people in our churches are in the workplace in some form (including stay-at-home moms, volunteers, and others who are not paid in money for their work). I also assume we already affirm that all believers are in full-time ministry (service) to Christ, and that the various fields in which non-ordained people work are just as much ministry as the pastorate and the mission field (Colossians 3:23-24).

Here are some additional reasons economics should be important to pastors:

- To preach and teach the Bible accurately when it addresses matters of work and economics (which it does regularly),
- To fully understand the dominion mandate of Genesis 1-2,
- To productively help the poor without generating dependency, and
- To help people in the marketplace see how God is forming them spiritually.

The Beginning of Economics in Genesis

From the beginning, we learn that God created the world and called it good, making the material world fundamentally good (Genesis 1:31). He further entrusted human beings with dominion over the Earth – giving them both the *privilege* of enjoying the benefits of the material world, but also the *responsibility* for caring for the world. We also learn that, from the beginning, God has implanted his wisdom into the world, and given human beings the necessary freedom and tools – God-given intelligence, initiative, and creativity – to uncover and apply his wisdom for their benefit (Proverbs 8:22-31).

This is all a part of the responsible exercise of dominion over creation that brings innovation and productivity to benefit humankind. British economist Sir Brian Griffiths rightly sees in the dominion mandate that: "Man has been created with an urge to control and harness the resources of nature in the interests of the common good, but he is subject to his accountability to God as a trustee to preserve and care for it. This process is precisely what an economist would refer to as *responsible wealth creation*."[89] The dominion mandate reflects an essential part of mankind being made in God's image, giving us an innate inclination to utilize the created world for productive purposes. In creation, God is portrayed as a worker (Genesis 1:31) who continues working to sustain his world. His creativity, initiative, and resourcefulness displayed in creation are also traits that have been given to human beings by virtue of being made in his image. Responsible human dominion over creation involves exercising these creative qualities.

In addition, since the image of God is fundamentally relational, this suggests that work is intended to be embedded in relationships. That is, the creation of male and female together to reflect the image of God has implications not only for procreation, but also for work. We are made for cooperation and relationships as we fulfill the dominion mandate, which suggests that economic systems enable those aspects of the image of God to flourish. In Genesis, God ordained work as good and as a primary means by which to accomplish dominion (Genesis 2:15); though as a result of sin, work was corrupted and made more difficult (Genesis 3:16).

Economics in the Old Testament

The Bible begins to address economics more frequently in Old Testament law. Israel became a nation "under God" which required a set of guidelines resembling a constitution. Many of these guidelines in Old Testament law involve economics. The purpose of Israel's constitution was to show how the Israelites could model God's righteousness in the way they lived together as a nation – that is, how they could become a "holy nation" (Exodus 19:5-6).

When it came to economics, the Israelites accomplished this in two ways. One was to make sure that their society was fair – that when people made exchanges, they did so without engaging in fraud or cheating each other. For example, the law mandated that the scales used to weigh measures of goods were accurate (Leviticus 19:35-36, Deuteronomy 25:13-16). The law assumed that individuals could legitimately own and accumulate property, since laws prohibiting theft and fraud only make sense if private property is legitimate. But the law also made it clear that God is the ultimate owner of everything (Leviticus 25:23).

The second way that the Israelites ensured they were a "holy nation" in economics was to care for the poor properly (Deuteronomy 15:1-11; 26:12-13). Their society assumed that people were responsible for taking care of themselves and their families. Old Testament law focused on how to provide for those who could not provide for themselves – that was the definition of the poor.

---

[89] Brian Griffiths, "The Creation of Wealth: The Christian Case for Capitalism," (Downers Grove, Ill.: Intervarsity Press, 1984), 52-53. Emphasis in the original.

The law structured many aspects of economic life to ensure that the poor were not without opportunity to take care of themselves. For example, the law mandated a tradition known as "gleaning," which permitted the poor to make their way through another's agricultural field and gather some of the produce for themselves (Leviticus 19: 9-10). The law also provided for a right of property redemption, so that the poor who had met misfortune could have renewed opportunity to make a living themselves (Leviticus 25:25-28). There was the tradition of the year of Jubilee, which returned land to its original owners every 50th year (Leviticus 25: 8-12). (There is no evidence that such a radical tradition was ever followed, and there is substantial debate about both its original intention and its contemporary significance.)

The law also set forth the Sabbath tradition, mandating a regular day of rest from work and grounding it in the original creation account. One of the main purposes for this was to help the people trust God to provide for them through the other six days of work each week (Exodus 20: 8-11; Deuteronomy 5:12-15). The law was concerned both about the overall goals of economic life – to provide for fair dealings and take care of the poor – as well as the means to accomplish those goals, with laws such as gleaning, redemption, and Jubilee.

God's heart for the poor is revealed throughout the Psalms and other poetic literature in the Old Testament. The marginalized, vulnerable, and oppressed occupy a special place in the heart of God, because he is their only defender and advocate. For example, Psalm 10:17-18 says, "You hear, O Lord, the desire of the afflicted; you encourage them and you listen to their cry, defending the fatherless and oppressed, in order that man, who is of the earth, may terrify no more." Similarly, in Psalm 82:2-4, God mandates caring for the poor and protecting them from those who would do them harm: "Defend the cause of the weak and fatherless; maintain the rights of the poor and oppressed. Rescue the weak and needy, deliver them from the hand of the wicked."

The wisdom literature, especially Proverbs, echoes this concern for the poor and oppressed. In fact, a community's care for the poor is considered an indication of how they value God: "He who oppresses the poor shows contempt for their Maker, but he who is kind to the needy honors God" (Proverbs 14:31, see also Proverbs 17:5 and 19:17). The prophets routinely and forcefully spoke out against oppression, economic injustice, and exploitation of the poor. They considered taking care of the poor a strong indicator of a person's (and the nation Israel's) spiritual health (Isaiah 58:6-7), even making a strong connection between compassion for the poor and genuinely knowing God (Jeremiah 22:16)! The prophets considered this neglect of the poor a serious violation of the law, and it was one of the symptoms of the major disease afflicting Israel: it was an abandonment of God for the worship of idols and false gods (Ezekiel 16:48; Amos 2:6-7 and 4:1, Micah 2:2-9, Habakkuk 2:6-12).[90]

Another important aspect of caring for the poor comes out of the wisdom books – that of *individual responsibility for prosperity*. These books repeatedly make the connection between diligence, hard work, initiative, and prosperity. For example, "lazy hands make a man poor, but diligent hands bring wealth" (Proverbs 10:4-5). This is part of a broader point made throughout the wisdom literature: a person's individual moral character (or to put it another way, adherence to the way of wisdom) determines the path that person's life takes. The fool, or one who lacks wisdom and character, typically ends up with a life of calamity, but the wise person, who has a well-developed character, typically ends up with a life of prosperity and well-being.

Of course, the proverbs are rules of thumb and not legal guarantees from God, so there are exceptions to this general pattern. There are poor saints and rich idiots! And sometimes the poor are poor because they are the victims of injustice (Proverbs 13:23). The Bible does not teach anything like a "prosperity theology" in which God always automatically rewards righteousness with material wealth. Even the Proverbs acknowledge that wealth doesn't last forever (Proverbs 27:24).

The general pattern in the Bible, however, is that prosperity is a matter of personal responsibility – namely, hard work, diligence, and perseverance (Proverbs 13:11; 14:23; 16:26; 20:13; 28:19, 20, 22, 25). The emphasis seems clear: individual responsibility, a strong work ethic, and other "entrepreneurial" character traits such as initiative and perseverance are critical to a life of economic prosperity. By contrast, the proverbs illustrate this with the portrait of the sluggard (Proverbs 19:24; 26:15; 22:13; 26:13; 24:30-34).

As important as these character traits are, it is also important to recognize that a person's prosperity is ultimately a blessing from God. This was more obvious in the agricultural economy of the ancient world. People were dependent on natural forces such as rainfall to have a sufficient harvest. But it is no less true in our information-based economy today. The proverbs indicate that it's the blessing of God that makes a person prosperous (Proverbs 10:22), and that God is the one who enables us to enjoy the fruit of our labors. He says that it's a good thing that we can enjoy life as his good gift (Ecclesiastes 2:24-25, 5:18-20).

Economics in the New Testament

In the New Testament, Jesus takes up where the prophets left off. The poor were just as important to Jesus as they were to the prophets. When the followers of

---

[90] Other symptoms of the disease of idolatry include various forms of violent crime (Habakkuk 2:8, 17), perversion of the justice system (mainly through bribery), and rampant sexual immorality.

John the Baptist (who was in prison at the time) asked Jesus if he was indeed the Messiah who was to come, he answered in terms that could have been taken directly from the prophets. He put it like this: "Go back to John [the Baptist] and tell him what you have seen and heard – the blind see, the lame walk, the lepers are cured, the deaf hear, the dead are being raised to life and the good news is being preached to the poor" (Matthew 11:4-5). The evidence that Jesus was who he claimed to be extended beyond his miracles to the identities of the beneficiaries of those miracles – the poor, marginalized, and vulnerable.

Similarly, when he spoke of final judgment and what would separate his true followers from the pretenders, he made it clear that how someone treats the poor is a critical indication of a person's spiritual maturity. This is likely what Jesus meant when he referred to the hungry and the needy by saying, "I tell you the truth, when you did it to the least of these my brothers, you were doing it to me" (Matthew 25:40).

Jesus didn't just talk about how important it was to take care of the poor, he modeled it too. Not counting the 12 disciples, Jesus spent the majority of his time with the outcasts of society – lepers, tax collectors, prostitutes, and the poor. He spent little time with those who were highly esteemed by the culture, such as the religious leaders and the rich. He valued the poor for who they were, and told people that they too should highly esteem the poor.

For example, he said: "When you put on a banquet, don't invite your friends, brothers, relatives and rich neighbors. For they will invite you back and that will be your only reward. Instead, invite the poor, the crippled, the lame and the blind. Then at the resurrection of the righteous, God will repay you for inviting *those who could not repay you*" (Luke 14:12-14). It's precisely because they cannot repay you in any way that serving the poor has great value. It models something very important about our relationship to God – his unconditional, no-strings-attached love for each of us – regardless of what we can repay him (obviously, nothing!).

Consistent with the message of the wisdom literature, many of Jesus' parables were drawn from the everyday world of work and economic life. The use of these parables also affirms the other main emphasis of the Old Testament when it comes to economics: the notion of personal responsibility for one's own material support. For example, the Parable of the Sower compares a person's reception of the kingdom of God to scattering seed among different types of soils (Matthew 13:1-23), and the Parable of the Wheat and Tares is about a field that produces mixed results despite the best efforts of the owner (Matthew 13:24-30). Other parables compare God's kingdom to fishing (Matthew 13:47-52), tending sheep (Luke 15:1-7), and shrewd business management (Luke 16:1-9).

Jesus also compares the Kingdom to business, in which resources are effectively put to use in order to generate a profit. The well-known Parable of the Talents assumes that it's legitimate to seek a profit and to work hard to deploy a person's financial resources to make that happen (Matthew 25:14-30; Luke 19:11-26), again emphasizing the notion of personal responsibility in continuity with the Old Testament. It would also seem to assume that accumulating wealth is not intrinsically a problem. Obviously, those who accumulate wealth must be careful to avoid the error of the rich fool, who put his trust in his wealth instead of God (Luke 12:13-21).

The early church carried on Jesus' pattern of caring for the poor and marginalized. They cared for the poor mainly through their extraordinary generosity, following Jesus' mandate to share freely with those in need (Luke 10:25-37; 12:33). They could not rely on the state to care for their poor, since the church was a persecuted minority in the Roman Empire and there were not many public mechanisms to take care of the poor. And many of the early followers of Jesus were quite poor themselves. We see this extraordinary generosity in action in Acts 2:42-47. The early church is described as "sharing everything they had." They even sold their personal possessions and property in order to meet the needs of the church.

It should be noted that this was a purely voluntary sharing of their material goods and not a pattern for the *forced* redistribution of goods characteristic of socialism. That's not to say that all redistribution of wealth is necessarily wrong, only that Acts 2 does not provide a basis for an economic arrangement like socialism. One major difference between socialist systems and the early church is that the *state* owns most of the means of production. Further, there was no forced renunciation of property in the early church. But there was unprecedented openhandedness with their goods to meet needs that arose. It may be that part of the reason for this was their belief that Jesus was returning to consummate his kingdom within their lifetimes.

In addition, after the day of Pentecost, in which 3,000 new believers were added to the church, many of them stayed in Jerusalem to learn more about Jesus. This put an extraordinary burden of hospitality on the church, which they met with amazing and Spirit-generated openhandedness. The main reason for their generosity, however, was their personal transformation by the message of Jesus. Acts 2 provides a model for this kind of personal liberality, but has little to say about economic systems themselves.[91]

As in the Old Testament, self-support and personal responsibility were assumed in the early church. Self-interest was not condemned, but affirmed and balanced

---

[91] To read more on the sharing of resources in the early church, see Justo L. Gonzales, "Faith and Wealth: A History of Early Christian Ideas on the Origin, Significance, and Use of Money" (New York: Harper Collins, 1990), 79-86.

by concern for the interests of others (Philippians 2:4). The responsibility for providing for your own needs and needs of your family was taken very seriously. The Apostle Paul encouraged a life of diligence in order to provide for self and family (1 Thessalonians 4:11-12), and cautioned those who were not willing to work when he said, "Those unwilling to work will not get to eat" (2 Thessalonians 3:13). He meant that if someone is not willing to work, he or she does not have any claim on the generosity of others. Paul modeled such a life of self-support, even while planting churches, so that he would not be a financial burden on the community. He strongly commanded idle people to "settle down and earn their own living" (2 Thessalonians 3:11-12). He stated this even more strongly when he counseled Timothy that "those who won't care for their relatives, especially those in their own household, have denied the true faith" (1 Timothy 5:8). This kind of personal responsibility for self-support is consistent throughout the Bible, while making room for generosity and provision for those who cannot care for themselves.

In "The Virtues of Capitalism: The Moral Case for Free Markets," my co-author and I provided a summary of some of the main elements of the Bible's teaching on economic life:

1. The material world is intrinsically good because it's God's good creation, though it is marred by sin.

2. God owns the world's economic resources, and human beings are trustees of those resources, responsible for their careful and productive use.

3. Responsible wealth creation is integrally connected with the dominion mandate and with human beings being made in the image of God.

4. Work/economic activity is fundamentally good, ordained by God.

5. Human beings who are capable of working are responsible for supporting themselves and their dependents.

6. The community is responsible for helping support those who are unable to work.

7. Human beings are not to exploit the economically vulnerable, but to help them support themselves.[92]

The Modern Economy

When it comes to economics, the world of the Bible and today's global economy are totally different. In the Bible, most people made their living in agriculture or in a modest trade (such as Jesus' carpentry business or his disciples' fishing business). It was difficult to get ahead financially; most people were stuck in the

---

[92] Austin Hill and Scott B. Rae, "The Virtues of Capitalism: The Moral Case for Free Markets" (Chicago: Northfield Publishing, 2010).

socioeconomic station in life into which they were born. There were not many "rags to riches" stories in the ancient world. Most of the rich became wealthy through some sort of corruption, usually through abuse of political power (like the tax collectors) or exploiting the vulnerable. It was in this context that Jesus said that it's harder for a rich man to enter the kingdom of God than for a camel to go through the eye of a needle, since becoming rich usually involved very shady and corrupt practices (Matthew 19:24).

But that's not all that is different. In the ancient world, no one except the very rich retired. You simply worked until you were not able to work any longer. At that point, you relied on your extended family to take care of you. In addition, there was not much saving or investing for the long term, since most goods were perishable and there was nothing like today's stock market or other investment vehicles. This was one reason it made so little sense for the rich fool to build bigger barns in which to store his crops (Luke 12:13-21).

Further, the lot of the poor was very difficult, since the communities charged with caring for them often failed to discharge their responsibility. This left the needy in a very precarious position. The poor in the ancient world probably had more in common with the desperately poor in Third World nations than they did with the poor in developed nations.

Finally, there is a big difference between the global economy of today and the local economy of the ancient world. In biblical times, there was some modest international trade, but most economic activity took place in the local community. There was nothing resembling the global supply chain or the worldwide customer base that many companies have today.

Most of these differences between the ancient world and our developed economy help us understand why the vast majority of people in the ancient world (in fact, for most of history until the Industrial Revolution) were very poor, had little, if any, socioeconomic mobility, and were dependent on subsistence level agriculture or modest trades to make a living. There was not much economic *flourishing* because there was no economic system in place to enable the average person to flourish, as opposed to merely survive. Economic systems are important because they can either inhibit or unleash the creative and innovative capacities of people made in God's image.

Economic systems that enlarge the freedom of human beings to exercise their entrepreneurial traits, cooperate in using their gifts, support their households, and personally help care for the poor are closer to the biblical ideal than those that inhibit these activities. When considering this, we must remember that we can apply the Bible to this question *only for general principles, not specific policies.*[93] To put it another way, we look to the Bible for the ends (i.e., purposes) of the economic system more than for the means of accomplishing those ends.

The Bible is clear about some of the ends that a just economic system should accomplish. First, the economic system should *maximize the opportunities for human beings to exercise creativity, initiative, and innovation* – what we might call "human capital." These are a key part of what it means for human beings to exercise dominion over creation (to put the resources of the world to responsible and productive use) and be made in God's image.

A second clear end of the economic system is *to provide a means for human beings to support themselves and their dependents* – that is, to provide access to the world's productive resources. Market-oriented economics provide the best means for the most people to achieve self-support and lift themselves out of poverty within a context of social stability characterized by the rule of law and a strong moral culture. The evidence that market systems tend to accomplish this is overwhelming, as roughly 80 percent of the world's population has risen out of dire poverty in the past generation due, in large part, to the opening up of participation in the global market economy.[94]

A third end of the economic system is that *it must take care of those who cannot take care of themselves.* It must provide a safety net for the poor. Market-oriented economics provides the resources necessary for all economic assistance to the poor, whether through personal giving (which comes out of workers' paychecks), church and nonprofit programs (from contributions that come out of workers' paychecks), or public programs (from taxes that come out of workers' paychecks). Personal, church-based, nonprofit, and government assistance all require considerable productive wealth creation to sustain them.

More importantly, market-oriented economics provides opportunities for the poor to rise out of poverty. Through a combination of their own efforts and assistance from others, they can develop into people who are able to support themselves as participants in the system, and no longer live as recipients of charity. This upholds their human dignity, which is more important than money. Market economies provide opportunities for people to grow in this way.

---

[93] Griffiths, "The Creation of Wealth," 45.

[94] Maxim Pinkovskiy and Xavier Sala-i-Martin find that the number of people living on a dollar per day or less dropped 80 percent between 1970 and 2006 ("Parametric Estimations of the World Distribution of Income," National Bureau of Economic Research, October 2009, http://www.nber.org/papers/w15433.); other researchers come up with different figures, but all agree that the drop in global poverty has been significant.

Conclusion

There is much more to spiritual life than our eternal destiny. Life on this side of eternity matters greatly. This is reflected in the fact that Jesus had more to say about money and economics than he did about eternity. If we refuse to separate the sacred from the secular, and affirm that all of life is spiritual, then there are few, if any, areas of our spiritual lives that are not impacted by economics. Pastors need to understand the meaning and purpose of these systems and practices in order to help people develop spiritually and live the way God wants them to.

REFLECTION QUESTIONS

1. What connection does Rae find between the "dominion mandate" (or cultural mandate) in creation, responsibility, and economics?

2. Recall the seven "main elements of the Bible's teaching on economic life" Rae lists. How do the people in your congregation and throughout your community encounter these economic issues on a daily basis? How can you help them develop wisdom about these issues?

3. Rae identifies three ways we can apply biblical principles to the modern economy. What do you think of them? Would these principles help people better understand the meaning of their lives in their communities?

Made for
DIGNITY

P.J. Hill

Justice demands a concern for the dignity of every individual. Just as each person's work is broken, the social system of the economy is broken. Just as we must help individuals find hope and meaning in the midst of toil, we must help our cultures find justice and dignity in a world marred by cronyism, materialism, debt, and dependence. As P.J. Hill argues in this eye-opening essay, the spread of the idea that every human being is made in the image of God was one of the most important events in *economic* history. Economic rights once reserved for the elite were extended to all, leading to an unprecedented explosion of economic growth – and with it, a whole new set of challenges and opportunities for the church. If pastors intend to bear witness for justice in our world, they must set aside easy answers and grapple with complex, ambiguous questions. Renewing our public commitment to the equal dignity of all human beings is one of the most important challenges the church faces in the coming generation.

P.J. Hill is professor emeritus of economics at Wheaton College. He is enjoying retirement in Manhattan, Mont., where he ran his family's cattle ranch each summer while teaching economics at Wheaton for 25 years. He holds a Ph.D. in economics from the University of Chicago. Hill also serves on the national advisory committee of the Oikonomia Network. If you like this essay, check out his book "The Not So Wild, Wild West." In spite of a century of mythology about the lawless frontier, he argues that prosperity came to the American West only when reliable and impartial enforcement of contract and property rights – in short, the rule of law – was imposed. His other books include "The Technology of Property Rights," "The Political Economy of the American West," "The Birth of a Transfer Society," and "Who Owns the Environment?"

If pastors want to help people understand their world, their culture, and their work in a moral and spiritual way, they need to understand the spiritual sources and significance of economic growth. The rise of sustained economic growth in the modern world is one of the most dramatic developments in all history. And if pastors are not content simply to help people *understand* their world, but actually want to help people promote human flourishing, it is all the more important that pastors understand what economic growth is, what its effects are, and what tends to sustain or undermine it.

There is an inseparable connection between human dignity and economic growth. At the most immediate level, growth has allowed large numbers of people to overcome material poverty in a sustainable way. This has never happened anywhere before the emergence of the modern economy.

Figure 1

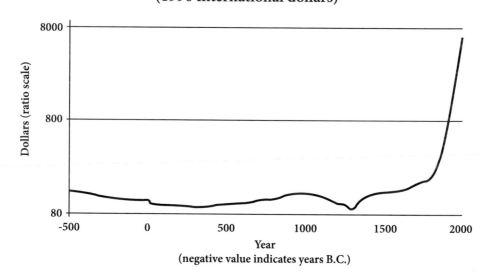

Per capita Annual World GDP, 500 B.C. - 2000 A.D.
(1990 international dollars)

Source: Victor Claar, "The Urgency of Poverty and the Hope of Genuinely Free Trade," Journal of Markets and Morality 16, no. 1 (Spring 2013): 274. Calculated from J. Bradford DeLong, "Estimates of World GDP, One Million B.C.-Present," 1998, http://delong.typepad.com/print/20061012_LRWGDP.pdf.

But the connection runs deeper than that. As we will see, one of the most important historical factors contributing to the emergence of economic growth was the increasing recognition of equal human dignity. As ordinary people gained protection for human rights that had previously been reserved for social elites, the legal and social conditions emerged for economic growth to occur.

Economic growth has substantially increased human well-being in many parts of the world. The graph on the opposite page demonstrates what has happened to world income per person since 1,000 B.C. Early estimates are based upon fragmentary data, but there is little question that for almost all of recorded history, the basic lot of humankind was to live in relative poverty. Of course, relative poverty doesn't mean that all people were just at the level of subsistence, nor does it mean that there were not some people in some societies that were able to accumulate substantial wealth. Nevertheless, until 1800, no economy had experienced substantial enough economic growth to raise the standard of human well-being for ordinary people much beyond the basic necessities of life.[95]

There are other indicators of economic well-being besides the single measure of income per person, and those also showed little change for most of history until a sudden takeoff about 200 years ago. The world average life expectancy in 1820 was 26 years of age, about the same as it had been over the previous 1,000 or 2,000 years.[96] Today, the world average life expectancy is 70, according to the World Health Organization.

Other, more specific indicators also help one to understand the dramatic changes in lifestyle. In today's developed world, one hour of work by the average person earns enough money to pay the electric company for 300 days' worth of light sufficient for reading; in 1800, an hour of work earned enough to purchase candles or lamp oil sufficient for only 10 minutes of reading light.[97] The impact of this single advance on our daily lives is enormous – very few activities used to happen after sunset because light was too expensive. More recent data also point to dramatic economic changes. In 1900, the average American spent 76 percent of his or her income on food, clothing, and shelter. Only 37 percent of that person's income is used for those purposes today.[98]

Casual observation may be the most powerful tool for most of us. Anyone from a developed economy who travels to other parts of the world is struck by the

---

[95] The date 1800 is chosen as an approximation of when sustained economic growth began. There is controversy among economic historians as to the precise date, but there is general agreement that it occurred between 1750 and 1820.

[96] Angus Maddison, "The World Economy: A Millennial Perspective" (Paris: Development Centre of the Organisation for Economic Co-operation and Development, 2001), 30.

[97] Matt Ridley, "The Rational Optimist: How Prosperity Evolves" (New York: Harper, 2010), 34-35.

[98] Ibid., 34.

poverty of much of the population. When seeing people living in what we might consider a state of relative deprivation, we should remember that their living conditions represent how most of the world lived for most of history.

Thinking about this also reveals a problem with Figure 1. Measuring world income per person fails to consider how the increases in income since 1800 are distributed. The distributions are very uneven. In fact, the period from 1800 to the present has been labeled by some as "The Great Divergence" for this very reason.

Several questions come to mind when one looks at the "hockey stick" layout of Figure 1, which depicts several thousand years with no substantial economic growth, then a sudden takeoff that has changed economic life in unbelievable ways for a substantial portion of the world.[99] First, why did growth occur after so many years of stagnation? Second, where did this growth first begin, and why did it start in those places? And finally, why are some parts of the world still quite poor?

Christianity and the "Institutional Revolution"

The most powerful explanation for the beginning of substantial economic growth is change in the institutional framework – the basic rules and mores that govern society. It is generally agreed that the first economic takeoff occurred in England and the Netherlands in the late 18th and early 19th century, as they were the first to experience an institutional revolution that overturned ancient ways of structuring society (Acemoglu and Robinson 2012; North, Wallis, and Weingast 2009; McCloskey 2010). Countries that did not adopt these institutional changes until later fell behind dramatically in terms of economic growth.

The beginning of economic growth in Western Europe seems a bit odd, particularly given the advanced technology and early economic flourishing that occurred elsewhere in the world. For instance, China, under the Song Dynasty (960-1279) was at the forefront of technological change.[100] The Chinese invented gunpowder, the compass, and porcelain, and they were able to produce pig iron at a rate not met in England for another 700 years. They even had a power-driven

---

[99] Just because there has been dramatic growth in income per person since 1800 does not mean that life has improved on all dimensions since then. Terrible and deadly wars have been fought, and there have been numerous atrocities and economic disruptions. On the other hand, the fact that incomes did not rise for most of history should not be interpreted as an indication that nothing of interest happened during that period. Great civilizations rose and fell, beautiful works of art were created, complex physical structures were erected, and music and literature flourished in many times and places.

[100] Daron Acemoglu and James A. Robinson, "Why Nations Fail: The Origins of Power, Prosperity, and Poverty" (New York: Crown Publishers, 2012), 231.

spinning machine 500 years before the English.[101] In 1500, income per person in China was very close to that in Europe.[102]

Another region where one might have expected the economic takeoff to occur is the Middle East. According to Timur Kuran:

> A millennium ago, around roughly the tenth century, the Middle East was an economically advanced region of the world, as measured by standard of living, technology, agricultural productivity, literacy or institutional creativity. Only China might have been more developed.[103]

Like China, however, reasonable prosperity and economic power in the Middle East did not ensure ongoing growth. Rodney Stark argues that the influence of Christianity was crucial for substantial growth because of its embrace of reason and logic.[104] Since the Christian faith sees reason as a gift from God, it is appropriate to apply logical thought processes to matters of technology and economic organization. Thus, largely through the influence of the Scholastics,[105] reason became an integral part of Western culture. A major influence on technological change was the belief that God created an ordered world, and it was thus appropriate to discover that order.

Christianity's view of history as linear rather than circular was another important factor leading to economic growth. It strongly encouraged the active application of technology to improve the world, relieve suffering, and serve human needs. Most cultures have historically believed that human history is nothing but the same thing repeated over and over again; this tends to undermine the motivation to work diligently to put technological advancements to good use. What's the point? The Christian view of history legitimized the study of the past and the envisioning of a new future of greater human flourishing.[106]

Stark's explanation is powerful, but not complete. Some parts of Christian Western civilization developed more rapidly than others, as shown by the considerable evidence that England and the Netherlands led the way in the economic takeoff. These countries led because they were the first to adopt, in the words of Acemoglu and Robinson, inclusive institutions rather than extractive ones. For these authors,

---

[101] David S. Landes, "Dynasties: Fortunes and Misfortunes of the World's Great Family Businesses" (New York: Viking, 2006), 5.

[102] Acemoglu and Robinson, "Why Nations Fail," 231.

[103] Timur Kuran, "Why the Middle East is Economically Underdeveloped: Historical Mechanisms of Institutional Stagnation," Journal of Economic Perspectives 18, no. 3 (Summer 2004): 71-90.

[104] Rodney Stark, "The Victory of Reason: How Christianity Led to Freedom, Capitalism, and Western Success" (New York: Random House, 2005).

[105] "The Scholastics were Christian thinkers who were influential from the 11th through the 15th century." Greg Forster, "The Contested Public Square: The Crisis of Christianity and Politics" (InterVarsity Press: Downers Grove, 2008), 84.

[106] Stark, "The Victory of Reason."

inclusive institutions are made up of the rule of law, contract enforcement, well-defined property rights, and a political system that is reasonably open. By contrast, extractive institutions enable the powerful elite to capture wealth at the expense of the masses. McCloskey adds belief structures to the list of important influences. She argues that England and the Netherlands had belief structures that accorded much more dignity to the bourgeoisie – the middle class, which had the most untapped potential for economic productivity – thus encouraging entrepreneurial activity and economic growth.[107]

The above explanations also reveal why neither China nor the Middle East were the launching pad for economic growth. China's rulers were clearly autocratic, and economic growth was viewed as disruptive and dangerous for the ruling elite.[108] In the Middle East, Islamic law had a substantial influence on institutional development. Although it was well suited for commercial activity in the early part of the second millennium, it did not allow for institutional innovation. Commerce changed, but Islamic law did not. In particular, the modern corporate form of production was made difficult because of the Quran's inheritance rules, and because the *waqf*, a private Islamic charitable structure, locked vast resources into a system unable to effectively provide what economists call "public goods." [109]

The Limited Access Order

Economic growth depends on the appropriate set of institutional conditions, along with the belief structure that brings such institutions into existence. Acemoglu and Robinson provide a detailed description of the positive effect of inclusive institutions and the debilitating impact of extractive ones. The most complete theory of institutional change and the best understanding of the rules and norms necessary for economic growth, however, comes from "Violence and Social Orders: A Conceptual Framework for Interpreting Recorded Human History," by Douglass North, John Wallis, and Barry Weingast.[110]

North, Wallis, and Weingast argue that violence is endemic to human social orders, and the fear of violence has been the underlying motivation for the basic structures of rules that have governed societies for almost all of history. People have been willing to live under regimes that do not fully respect their rights because these structures are better than living in a state of anarchy under the constant threat of violent plunder and attack. North, Wallis, and Weingast call these structures "the natural state" because they have been the predominant way of organizing societies for most of history.

---

[107] Deirdre McCloskey, "Bourgeois Dignity: Why Economics Can't Explain the Modern World" (Chicago: University of Chicago Press, 2010).

[108] Acemoglu and Robinson, "Why Nations Fail," 231-234.

[109] Kuran, "Why the Middle East is Economically Underdeveloped."

[110] North, Wallis, and Weingast, "Violence and Social Orders."

The natural state is a coalition of political and economic elites who provide support for each other's functions. The economic elites are protected from competition – in other words, they monopolize various economic activities. In return for protection of their monopoly, the producers support the political rulers. Thus, economic and political elites create a mutually reinforcing alliance of control over economic production and control of coercive power.

North, Wallis, and Weingast also call this the "limited access order" because the dominant coalition limits entry into both political and economic life. The coalition is only stable with a limited number of participants, and different people in different social roles live under different rules. Rather than one set of laws for all people, personal relationships are the basis for social organization.

This also means that personal exchange has been the dominant form of economic organization. Almost all economic exchange throughout history took place between people who knew one another. Moreover, exchange was not standardized for all people, but differed from person to person. If 100 people each walk into a store today and buy the same item, they all pay the same price for it. Modern exchange has been standardized and made impersonal. Under conditions of personal exchange in the limited access order, however, each person might pay a different price and get a different product, because different people have different social statuses, and economic exchange is an expression of personal relationships.

A key feature of the limited access order is the "pervasive sense that not all individuals were created or are equal."[111] The limited access order denies many members of society full access to means of production and opportunities for exchange. In other words, property rights are not secure for all citizens, and contract enforcement is uneven. This inequality is the basis for social and economic relationships. An important implication of this order is that the rule of law is not applied equally to all citizens.

The natural state, or limited access order, has taken many forms throughout history, with quite different coalitions in control at different times and places. Some that still exist today are fragile, and their order is transient. Some provide durable and stable state power. And some mature natural states, although still ruled by a dominant coalition, may practice a rule of law for the elites with reasonably well-articulated private and public law.

Despite the different forms of the natural state, it is important to remember that the control of violence is very important to most members of any society. People are willing to live under a ruling coalition that continually preys upon ordinary citizens because it is better than what seems to be the only other alternative: anarchy with ongoing violence. As a result, it's a world where ownership claims

---

[111] Ibid., 12.

are uncertain, inventors and entrepreneurs are scarce, and the general population lacks a strong drive to improve its economic situation. There is no assurance of property rights, so those who build better lives for themselves and their neighbors are unlikely to keep what they build; the powerful simply seize it. Without secure property and contract rights, economic producers will choose, whenever possible, to minimize the risk of having their property stolen or plundered. Such choices mean less productive activity occurs.

The Open Access Order and Economic Growth

A dramatic change occurred in Western Europe during 1400-1800.[112] In England and the Netherlands, an entirely different social order emerged – what North, Wallis, and Weingast call the open access order. They list several characteristics of this type of order:

1. A widely held set of beliefs about the inclusion of and equality for all citizens.

2. Unrestrained entry into economic, political, religious, and educational activities.

3. Support for organizational forms in each activity that is open to all (for example, contract enforcement).

4. Rule of law enforced impartially for all citizens.

5. Impersonal exchange.[113]

The above conditions are crucial for economic growth. Investment in new forms of production often requires a period of time before the investment produces a return. The rule of law and contract enforcement provide security for innovators. That security must extend to a wide group of citizens before it will broadly cultivate entrepreneurial energies and technological innovations in society.

Economic growth occurs when institutions encourage innovation, reward effort, and channel investments in productive endeavors. Thus, the natural state, or limited access order, erects substantial barriers to growth because of the uncertain nature of property rights. Entrepreneurial initiative is stifled because there are short time horizons for capturing returns on investments. Moving from personal to impersonal exchange expands the range of opportunities for people to benefit from economic exchange, because they can exchange with so many more people. It also increases the gains that can be made from specialization of labor, as there are more people to increase the diversity of forms of labor.

---

[112] Douglass North and Robert Paul Thomas, "The Rise of the Western World; a New Economic History" (Cambridge, University Press, 1973).

[113] North, Wallis, and Weingast, "Violence and Social Orders," 114.

Christianity and the Open Access Order

Political and economic change cannot be divorced from belief structures. The first requirement of the open access order – a commitment to the equality of all citizens – is foundational for the other parts of that order. Freedom of entry, contract enforcement, and the rule of law are all rooted in the moral equality of all members of a society. It is in this arena that the influence of Christianity is important.

The Christian concept of natural law, or moral laws, which can be discovered by the human intellect and applied to human relationships and orderings, was at the root of the institutional changes that led to economic growth. Natural law was most fully articulated by the Scholastics, although it was a part of religious thought for centuries. Thomas Aquinas (1225-1274) was one of the major contributors to the development of natural law. Others who followed Aquinas more fully developed the idea that moral laws as discoverable by the human intellect should be the basis of political organization.[114] A fundamental premise of natural law is the moral equality of all people, since all bear the image of God. It is this basic concept that is the intellectual grounding for the institutional details of North, Wallis, and Weingast's open access order. Hence, it is worth examining in more detail how the concept of the *imago Dei* influenced institutional development.

An important aspect in understanding how *imago Dei* influenced institutional development is the relationship of natural law to natural rights; the list of institutional conditions of North, Wallis, and Weingast depends heavily upon a well-articulated doctrine of human rights. For the purposes of this essay, I take the position that natural rights theory has the same basic roots as natural law theory. Both are grounded in a belief in the dignity of all humans.[115]

The church's natural law and natural rights doctrines were an important part of political thought long before the modern era, but they were more forcefully articulated and more successfully applied to cultural structures with the coming of the Protestant Reformation. One of Martin Luther's primary claims was the dignity of all humans, as expressed in his 1520 tract, "The Freedom of the Christian."[116] Because we all stand equal before God, human equality is divinely constructed, not humanly constructed. Luther did not develop a strong case for political freedom; in fact, after the Peasant's Revolt of 1525, he emphasized strong political authority as necessary for an orderly society. Nevertheless, his argument

---

[114] William of Ockham (1288-1348) was one of the later, influential Scholastics. His concept of natural law prescribed more limits on the use of power than did Thomas Aquinas. See Forster, "The Contested Public Square," 104.

[115] Brian Tierney, "The Idea of Natural Rights: Studies on Natural Rights, Natural Law, and Church Law, 1150-1625" (Atlanta: Scholars Press, 1997), 347.

[116] John Witte, "The Teachings of Modern Christianity on Law, Politics, and Human Nature" (New York: Columbia University Press, 2006), 50-51.

for freedom of conscience was an important first step in the development of more general human rights.

John Calvin (1509-1564) wrote eloquently about the importance of protecting other domains in life – including church, family, and commerce – from potentially selfish use of power in the hands of political rulers. This was another important step toward recognizing that people have political and economic rights. Theodore Beza (1519-1605), a reformer in the mold of Calvin, developed a more complete articulation of an appropriate political order that protected religious and economic liberty. For Beza, the right of revolution against tyrants was an important part of one's basic rights. An aristocratic Frenchman, he was expelled from the French Parliament when he converted to Protestantism. Throughout the 16th century, there was tension between advocates of individual liberty and those who wanted freedom for the religious authorities to deal with heretics. Because of French persecution of Protestant believers, Beza gradually developed a more robust theory of individual freedom based upon a contract theory of the state.[117]

Although Beza's writings represented new developments in political and religious thought, he drew upon centuries of Christian thinking. In the words of John Witte, "He called on five decades of Protestant and five centuries of Catholic teachings on law, politics, and society as well as the whole arsenal of classical and patristic sources."[118]

Emergence of the Open Access Order: The Netherlands

Although much of the early debate over religious liberty and individual rights occurred in France and Germany, the Netherlands fairly quickly became a hotbed for discussion over the importance of the image of God in formulating rules for the political order. Johannes Althusius (1557-1638) was probably the most important contributor to this debate. Althusius was an active pamphleteer, authoring numerous pieces on natural law and the liberties of individuals and groups.

Althusius started his theory of society and politics with an account of the state of nature – now human nature, and more particularly, the nature of persons as creatures and image bearers of God. God created humans as moral creatures, Althusius argued, with natural law written on their hearts and consciences and "an innate inclination," "hidden impulse," and "natural instinct" to be "just and law abiding." God created persons as rights holders, vested with natural sovereignty, rooted in the supernatural sovereignty of God, whose image each person bears upon birth.[119]

---

[117] John Witte, "The Reformation of Rights: Law, Religion, and Human Rights in Early Modern Calvinism" (Cambridge: Cambridge University Press, 2007), 129-131.

[118] Ibid., 89.

[119] Ibid., 182.

Throughout the 16th and 17th centuries, there was a gradual evolution toward an open access order in the Netherlands, and the concept of the moral equality of all people was an important driving force. The Joyous Entry of 1356, like the Magna Carta, provided a written basis for governance, and the Grand Privilege of 1477 provided a list of the ruler's duties and the rights of the people. Finally, in 1581, the Dutch Act of Abjuration declared Phillip II, King of Spain, Duke of Burgundy, and the Lord of the Netherlands, a tyrant who no longer was to be obeyed.

These formal changes in governance gave the Northern Provinces greater political freedom. With increased political freedom came more economic freedom, especially the freedom to enter trades, undertake manufacturing start-ups, and engage in transactions across time and space. Thus, the features of the open access order became more and more a part of Dutch economic life. Property rights were clearly defined and enforced. By 1500, manorial obligations were eliminated, and clear title to land was more the rule than the exception. Because of the economic and political freedom, an influx of foreigners arrived to ply their trades, and the local guilds were not powerful enough to stop them.[120] In the first part of the 17th century, one-third of Amsterdam's 100,000 residents were newly arrived foreigners.[121]

The state was not active in granting monopoly rights to particular producers. The freedom to form new businesses and to engage in trade without interference from the government meant increased specialization, bringing enormous increases in productivity and trade. Regional fairs became commonplace and served to reduce the transaction costs of trade. "A London merchant, for example, could purchase grain from the Baltic in these markets, seeing and retaining only a sample. The seller warranted that the delivered goods would be as good or better than the sample."[122] Of course, secure property rights and contract enforcement were crucial elements in such transactions. There were even futures markets and sale by grade. An active capital market developed, enabling investors to finance production and trade.

Emergence of the Open Access Order: England

In England, individual rights also evolved over time, a phenomenon that reduced the power of the natural state. The Magna Carta was signed in 1215, enforcing one of the first limitations of the power of the sovereign. In 1265, the first Parliament was elected. The next 400 years saw institutional evolution, with numerous changes in political power. When King Charles I came to the throne in 1625, he regarded Parliament as more a functionary of the Crown than a representative of the people and imposed taxes that supposedly required the assent of Parliament.

---

[120] North and Thomas, "The Rise of the Western World," 134.
[121] Stark, "The Vistory of Reason," 145.
[122] North and Thomas, 136.

He also persecuted the Puritans, driving many of them to the Netherlands and the American colonies.[123] When Charles called Parliament into session in 1640, after no meetings for 11 years, chaos ensued. Many of Charles' acts were revoked, civil and criminal jurisdiction was moved from the King's Court to common law courts, and power over all future taxation was claimed by Parliament. Charles retaliated by abolishing Parliament and attempting to arrest its leaders for treason; he was executed in 1649 after a public trial. A civil war erupted between the Crown loyalists and supporters of Parliament, with most Puritans siding with the parliamentary forces.

For a time, a somewhat democratic form of government ruled England. In 1660, the monarchy was restored under Charles II. His brother, James II, succeeded to the English throne a few years later, and he came into even worse conflict with Parliament. The Parliament revolted again in 1688 in the Glorious Revolution, firmly establishing parliamentary supremacy in the English constitution. The English Bill of Rights in 1689 was a major institutional move toward an open access order because it codified the rights of ordinary Englishmen.

This was a period of vibrant intellectual debate over the rights and duties of English citizens. Between 1640 and 1680, over 22,000 pamphlets, sermons, and tracts were published. The power of the sovereign, the protection of the rights of citizens, and the legitimacy of various laws and forms of governance were hotly contested.[124]

As in the Netherlands, a major part of the political debate over human rights was driven by the articulation of the dignity of all people. Two biblical doctrines were at the root of this perspective: Christ's death for all humans and the universality of the image of God in every person. These were important influences on the move to the rule of law, contract enforcement for all market participants, and the opening of occupations and businesses to a wider range of people.

Although numerous theologians and philosophers were involved in the debate, one of the most important figures was John Milton (1608-1674). According to Witte:

> [I]t was the great poet and political philosopher John Milton who provided the most interesting integrative theory of rights and liberty ... Milton argued that each person is created in the image of God with "a perennial craving" to love God, neighbor, and self. Each person has the law of God written on his or her heart, mind, and conscience and rewritten in Scripture, most notably in the Decalogue.[125]

---

[123] Witte, "The Reformation of Rights," 2007, 210.
[124] Ibid., 50-51.
[125] Ibid., 50-51.

Finally, a discussion of the influence of ideas on political and economic institutions is incomplete if it does not consider the influence of John Locke (1632-1704). Locke wrote from a Christian perspective (although his theological orthodoxy is the subject of some debate) and strove to find a way bring peace between different religious groups. Locke published his "Two Treatises of Government" in 1689, the same year that the English Bill of Rights was adopted. He offered what would later come to be the predominant understanding of the rights proclaimed in that document, developing more fully the conditions under which a revolution was justified. He also developed a much more complete theory of natural rights than was embodied in the 1689 Bill of Rights. Locke argued for the application of natural law to all equally, because all are equally God's creations, made to exercise dominion over the natural order.

Although it took several more decades for the institutional changes of the Glorious Revolution and the Bill of Rights to have a substantial impact on economic growth, the groundwork had been laid for an open access order. Over the 17th and 18th centuries, economic freedom shifted from the sole hands of political rulers to the hands of the citizens, and disapproval of government-granted monopolies grew. For example, the Royal African Company, chartered in 1660 under Charles II, lost numerous court cases over its monopoly rights and was finally abolished in 1689. The emergence of secure property rights aided innovators and entrepreneurs.

Property rights to land were codified and enforcement strengthened. The creation of the Bank of England in 1694 aided the development of financial markets and funding for industry. By 1800, numerous technological changes had dramatically lowered the costs of production. James Watt's improvements in the steam engine in the 1760s provided a major new source of power, which opened the door to many new economic developments. Advancements in metallurgy made possible the production of high-quality wrought iron, important for tools and machine parts. Numerous technological changes in textiles made cheap cloth available to people all over the world. British exports, primarily of textiles, doubled between 1780 and 1800.[126] It was more than just technological change, however. The "growth was based on the expansion of commerce, the growth of markets, and improvements in the allocation of resources."[127]

Again, it was the idea of the equality of all humanity that drove the institutional changes that permitted freedom of entry to all economic activity. The specialization and gains from trade that followed were at the heart of sustained economic growth.

---

[126] Acemoglu and Robinson, "Why Nations Fail," 205.
[127] Joel Mokyr, "The Enlightened Economy: An Economic History of Britain, 1700-1850" (New Haven: Yale University Press, 2009), 5.

It's Not All Protestantism:
Open Access Spreads to France and Spain

If England and the Netherlands were the first countries in Western Europe to experience economic growth, another question arises: What about other European nations that were powerful commercial entities, such as France and Spain? Why were they not among the first movers? Of course, one can argue that the move to a growth-enhancing institutional order was simply a function of the Protestant Reformation, and that Catholic countries experienced growth much later simply because they were Catholic.

That argument is too simple and does not fit the facts well. The Protestant Reformation was a part of France's religious experience. Moreover, as stated earlier, the Reformation ideas about natural law and the dignity of all people were deeply rooted in pre-Reformation religious thought. The Scholastics strongly articulated a doctrine of human equality, and the Late Scholastics (1350-1500), especially those in Spain, developed a whole body of thought that was supportive of commercial activity.

One has to turn to the economic and political conditions of France and Spain to understand why the institutional revolution was delayed in those countries. At the end of the Hundred Years War (1337-1453), France had driven the English out of territories in what is now northern France, and the government in Paris controlled the political and economic lives of French citizens.[128] The result was an absolutist regime with little institutional change.

France remained a mercantilist country, meaning its economic policies were focused on accumulating wealth at the expense of others through colonization, monopolization, restraint of trade, and other extractive policies, rather than seeking mutual gains through open trade. It had heavy taxes, a large bureaucracy, and strong protection of guilds and crown monopolies. The symbiosis of political and economic power meant that traditional means of production were protected by the state. For instance, its rules concerning the dyeing of cloth contained 317 articles.[129] The mercantilist policies were designed to generate income for the Crown. Institutional change was difficult because it threatened the stable relationship between favored producers and the ruling class. There was thus little opportunity to discuss new ways of ordering society, and Christian thought had little opportunity to influence the rules governing economic activity.

Spain in 1500 was the unquestioned economic powerhouse of Europe. Over the next 200 years, however, its economy failed to generate economic growth, and it declined rapidly relative to England and the Netherlands. Much of the Crown's

---

[128] Although English power was limited after 1500, what became modern France was not unified under one government for another 50 years.

[129] North and Thomas, "The Rise of the Western World," 126.

income came from the extraction of wealth from external sources. Spain had a large colonial network, especially in the New World, and the conquered regions and peoples there generated large amounts of income for the home country. Much of Spain's wealth from the New World literally came from seizing resources – digging up gold and other valuable commodities and shipping them across the Atlantic. The Low Countries also made payments to the Spanish Crown. The final source of government income came from the sheep industry, to which the Crown granted numerous special privileges that prevented increases in productivity in the rest of agriculture.

Property rights were insecure, and the dependence of the Crown on outside sources of income meant it had less reason to emulate the revolution in manufacturing and trade occurring in England and the Netherlands.[130] Evidence of the economic stagnation of Spain can be found in the move of people from the city to rural areas. In 1600, 20 percent of the Spanish population lived in urban settings, but by 1700, the number had fallen to 10 percent. This is the opposite of what happens in a growing economy.[131]

Like France, Spain did not have the general debate or institutional ferment of England and the Netherlands. This meant that basic concepts of human dignity had little opportunity to impact the institutional order. Those who cared about the moral equality of all people could not gain much of a hearing for their views or have much influence over institutional choices.

Conclusion

The takeoff in economic growth that began in parts of Western Europe around 1800 still impacts the everyday lives of millions of people. Our lives continue to transform as the growing economy creates a dynamic and ever more complex world. It represents one of the most important changes in all of history. It was the move to freedom of contract, open entry into occupations, rule of law, and impersonal exchange that created economic growth by giving people the opportunity to identify and specialize in the particular kinds of work that are most fruitful for them, and then realize even greater gains by exchanging their work with others around the world. At the center of it all is the view that human beings are morally equal, founded on the Christian idea of the *imago Dei*. This idea provided the intellectual and moral foundation for the institutional changes that have altered so many lives so profoundly.

---

[130] Ibid.

[131] Acemoglu and Robinson, "Why Nations Fail," 221.

REFLECTION QUESTIONS

1. The emergence of economic growth in modern history has had a transformative impact on every aspect of our culture. What are the moral and spiritual sources of economic growth? How do we see its effects in our communities?

2. Hill writes that an institutional revolution helped catalyze the Industrial Revolution. Where do we see the legacy of the institutional revolution in our culture today? Are some elements of that legacy in decline, and how is that of direct concern to pastors?

3. Compare the limited access order and the open access order. Where do you see signs that our culture today operates as a limited access order? As an open access order? Does the church have something to say about which is more just?

Made to

FLOURISH

All around us in our rapidly changing culture, people are asking: *What are we made for?* Do the things I do all day have real meaning? Do I put up with it all just so I can keep the house from falling down, pull some clothes on my body, and put food on the table – so I can keep surviving? And maybe squeeze in a few hours of leisure time when I get to do what I want? Is that what it's all for? If not, what's the point?

Meanwhile, inside the church, many people are asking: *What is pastoral ministry made for?* Is the changing world leaving the pastorate behind? What can be done about the millions of Christians who don't live as though they are Christians? When did Christianity become a leisure-time activity? How do we overcome the "get out of hell free card" faith we seem to be stuck with? Why does so much of what we do in church feel superficial? How do we help people encounter the weightiness of God, the enormity of his holiness, and the depth of his love?

The church and the culture cannot find the answers to their respective questions until they rediscover one another. Christians will rediscover what pastoral ministry is made for when they remember that *the life of faith is lived in the culture*, in the vocational world of work and economic exchange. We desperately need help – shepherds who will instruct and nurture us to live as disciples, equipped for fruitful work and economic wisdom. And the culture will find out what people are made for when it sees that life of faith being lived in vocation, as Christians go out and manifest their faith in the world of work and exchange.

Pastoral ministry is for making full-time disciples. If discipleship is a full-time job, disciples must do more than engage in religious works and make other disciples. They must go out into the world and work for the good of others. They must work to flourish in their own lives, to help their neighbors flourish, and to build flourishing communities.

As Dallas Willard put it:

> Because discipleship is a matter of learning to live, discipleship is a matter of our whole life. Its primary place is where we live: our home and our work. Discipleship is for the world, in the sense of ordinary life – *whole* life – and it only occurs in that world.
>
> Church activity, if it is to be successful in God's terms, is in support of such discipleship. The church is for discipleship, and discipleship is for the world as God's place. That is what the "Great Commission" of Matthew 28 plainly says. [132] (See also Colossians 3:17.)

"The church is for discipleship, and discipleship is for the world." For the world to do what? Flourish.

Flourishing doesn't mean becoming rich or powerful. It means being in right relationship with God and neighbor. It means becoming the person God made you to be, and achieving the fullest use of your potential to glorify God by loving him, loving others, and making the world a better place. For some, that may involve accomplishing extraordinary things; for others, it may involve enduring in godliness through great suffering and want. The amount of potential good you can accomplish in the world is not the point. What use you make of your potential for good – that's the point.

All of us are made to flourish in God's world. The gospel unlocks this flourishing, shining the light of God's holiness and love into the darkness of the world. With the gospel, we rediscover what it means to flourish and how to flourish in the presence and provision of God. We show this to our culture by how we live and work in our vocations.

As theological scholar Stephen Grabill puts it: "The church is the body of Christ, given as a gift for the life of the world." For the life of the world! For the lives of Christians in the world, as they live out their vocations, love their neighbors, empower the poor and oppressed, and live for the life of the world itself. We work for its flourishing and, in doing so, shine like stars in the darkness, giving light and bearing witness to hope.

Roll up your sleeves, pastors. There's wonderful work to be done!

---

[132] Dallas Willard, foreword to "Whole Life Transformation: Becoming the Change Your Church Needs," by Keith Meyer (Downers Grove: InterVarsity Press, 2010), 12.

FURTHER RESOURCES

Theology

- Darrell Cosden, "A Theology of Work: Work and New Creation" (2006)
- Tim Keller and Katherine Leary Alsdorf, "Every Good Endeavor: Connecting Your Work to God's Work" (2013)
- Amy L. Sherman, "Kingdom Calling: Vocational Stewardship for the Common Good" (2012)
- Tom Nelson, "Work Matters: Connecting Sunday Worship to Monday Work" (2011)

Pastoral Care

- Os Guinness, "The Call: Finding and Fulfilling the Central Purpose of Your Life" (2003)
- Lester DeKoster, "Work: The Meaning of Your Life: A Christian Perspective" (2010)
- Sebastian Traeger and Greg D. Gilbert, "The Gospel at Work: How Working for King Jesus Gives Purpose and Meaning to Our Jobs" (2014)
- Dallas Willard and Gary Black Jr. "The Divine Conspiracy Continued: Fulfilling God's Kingdom on Earth" (2014)
- "Theology of Work Project" | www.theologyofwork.org

Compassion

- Steve Corbett and Brian Fikkert, "When Helping Hurts: How to Alleviate Poverty Without Hurting the Poor – and Yourself" (2010)
- Robert Lupton, "Toxic Charity: How Churches and Charities Hurt Those They Help (And How to Reverse It)" (2011)
- "Poverty Cure Video Curriculum" (2012) | www.povertycure.org

Continued on next page

Common Good

- "Economic Wisdom Project: A Christian Vision for Flourishing Communities" (2014) | www.kffdn.org/files/economic-wisdom-project.pdf

- Kenman Wong and Scott Rae, "Business for the Common Good: A Christian Vision for the Marketplace" (2011)

- Jeff Van Duzer, "Why Business Matters to God: (And What Still Needs to Be Fixed)" (2010)

- "For the Life of the World: Letters to the Exiles Video Curriculum" (2014) | www.letterstotheexiles.com

---

Youth & Family

- Gene Edward Veith, "God at Work: Your Christian Vocation in All of Life" (2011) and "Family Vocation: God's Calling in Marriage, Parenting, and Childroom" (2012)

- Steve Garber, "The Fabric of Faithfulness: Weaving Together Belief and Behavior" (2007)

- Herman Bavinck, "The Christian Family" (2012)

For more resources, please visit www.madetoflourish.org

About the Editors:

Drew Cleveland served as a program associate in the Faith, Work, and Economics program at The Kern Family Foundation, and was a 2009 fellow of the Trinity Forum Academy. He is pursuing an M.Div. at Princeton Theological Seminary, where he hopes to continue exploring how to follow Jesus in the modern world.

Greg Forster, Ph.D., is a program director in the Faith, Work, and Economics program of The Kern Family Foundation. He directs the Oikonomia Network, a national learning community of theological educators and evangelical seminaries dedicated to helping pastors connect biblical wisdom, sound theology, and good stewardship to work and the economy. He is also the author of six books and numerous scholarly and popular articles, a senior fellow at the Friedman Foundation for Educational Choice, and a regular contributor to several online outlets.